Adolescent Hero in The Works of Katherine Anne Porter and J.D. Salinger

Adolescent Hero in The Works of Katherine Anne Porter and J.D. Salinger

Rashmi Gupta

ATLANTIC
PUBLISHERS & DISTRIBUTORS

Published by
ATLANTIC PUBLISHERS AND DISTRIBUTORS
B-2, Vishal Enclave, Opp. Rajouri Garden, New Delhi-27
Phones : 25413460, 25429987, 25466842

Sales Office
7/22, Ansari Road, Darya Ganj, New Delhi-110 002
Phones : 23273880, 23285873, 23280451
Fax : 91-11-23285873
web : www.atlanticbooks.com
e-mail : info@atlanticbooks.com

ISBN 81-269-0317-1

Typeset at
APD Computer Graphics, Delhi

Printed in India at
Mehra Offset Press, Delhi

DEDICATED TO

The Loving Memory
of
My Brother

Preface

Growing up for some adolescents is a source of anxiety. They dread relinquishing childhood dependency and assuming responsibility. Sometimes they feel completely overwhelmed by these problems. In these cases, previous blighting experiences make them hostile or excessively submissive.

From the birth an individual is influenced by the social environment and he influences it. The 'law of conditioning' plays a significant role in fashioning human personality. The influences of home, the freedoms and constraints of society and processes of conflict, co-operation, accommodation and isolation have distinct contribution in the process of conditioning. The social forces, social problems and social situations hamper or help an individual towards the realization of his aspirations. Many of the problems arise from gender discrimination and social set-up or structure.

It is against this backdrop that I have tried to assess the adolescent behaviour in the works of Katherine Anne Porter and J.D. Salinger. Katherine Anne Porter's later stories and J.D. Salinger's *The Catcher in the Rye* most appropriately suggest the modern predicament of alienation. Feeling isolated the hero distrusts truth, justice and love and negates everything conforming to a value-oriented society.

Salinger's main concern is with the dehumanizing effects of urbanization and technological developments on the psyche of an individual. The writer feels that an incessant striving for wealth, luxuries and comforts of technological civilization lead the individual to spiritual vacuity.

The individual in Ms. Porter's works desires to understand the past and compares it to the failures of modern man in a mechanized, chaotic world. Ms. Porter longs for the pastoral world of the past but mocks its inadequacy to meet the contemporary challenges. This paradox of illusion is essential to her art and philosophy of life.

I am highly indebted to the American Studies Research Centre, Hyderabad for meeting my requirements during this study. I owe thanks to the Library of the Panjab University, Chandigarh. My special thanks go to my husband and my sons for their patient bearing of all their neglect on my part.

The book would be highly useful not only to students and researchers of English Literature but also to students and researchers of Psychology and Psycho-Therapists.

RASHMI GUPTA

Contents

Introduction

It is true that the adolescent period is a time of great possibility; but it is also a time when one must pay a price for growing up. It is a time when the adolescent is deeply involved in the search through which each human being has sought to realize himself and to discover who he is, and what he might become, though there are many restraints from the society to keep him from realizing himself.

Hall thought of the period of adolescence as the critical stage of transition between the primitive and civilized person and christened it as the period of "storm and stress."[1] Erikson proposed that 'identity crisis' is the primary characteristic of adolescence. According to him, "For the adolescent, the problem is to achieve personal identity."[2] According to McCandless, "Adolescence is both a time of drastic change and a part of the continuous stream of human development. Adolescence is a bridge period, a time of shifting from one stage to another."[3]

The period of adolescence is a significant part of the human life-span. It is not only a period of preparation for adulthood or a passage from childhood to adulthood but it is also an important stage of the total developmental process in itself which is distinguished by specific characteristics. According to McCandless, "the attitudes and expectations of society also change sharply at pubescence. Such changes expose the adolescents to many frustrations and ambiguities that may increase aggression, blunt curiosity and anxiety."[4]

In this age of anxiety, adults themselves feel lost, confused and lack direction. So adolescents who are otherwise also driven by the thrust of puberty, are likely to repudiate adult values and may show meaningless and destructive behaviour. In this ever-changing society, we must therefore expect, a constantly changing response on the part of the adolescents. Further, we must anticipate additional uncertainty among adolescents because, within a changing society, different adults are sure to take up different attitudes towards the coming generation which will make it even harder for the adolescents to interpret what society expects of them.

As W.D. Wall has pointed out in *The Adolescent Child,* society today speaks to adolescents with many and often discordant voices. In adolescence, an individual is faced with a greater variety of new experiences than at any other time and he usually is less well prepared to meet these than at any other time.[5]

One of the paradoxes of the adolescent age is that the adolescent seeks independence, yet he wants also to be dependent on some older persons for help and support. Apart from pressures from within, his confusion stems from the difficulty in resolving the issue between authority and freedom. There are findings supporting the idea that democratic procedures promote a child's development better than autocratic procedures. But then there is uncertainty about what it means to be democratic. Whatsoever might be the conditions, there is reason to believe that at present there are many adolescents who have been exposed to more than the usual amount of confusion and inconsistency.

To understand the adolescents we need to study his inner life—his experience of his existence as a separate self, his psychological states, impressions, thoughts, feelings and desires. As children grow older, their quest for meaning increases. There are many who learn that it is not good to inquire too much into the meaning of things, yet for some who are suspicious of many things, it is very painful to discover that they are considered a very unreasonable and demanding, sometimes even abnormal. The self, being the most essential property of each adolescent's life, it is the centre of his purposes, hopes and strivings. If there is meaning in an adolescent's life, it is within himself that he realizes it.

Blos comments that modern society progressively tends to place a heavy burden of self-determination on the adolescent's shoulders: "The vacuum of institutionalized adolescence in Western society thus allows...a high degree of personality differentiation and individuation, since there are no obligatory models."[6] Weiner quotes Hall as writing thus in 1904: "The teens are emotionally unstable and pathetic." It is the age of inevitable turmoil in which the major predictable feature of a young person's behaviour is his unpredictability. It is characterized by emotionalism. Almost all later psychoanalytic writing has supported this view. Anna Freud's well-known description of adolescence is strikingly similar to that of G. Stanley Hall:

> Adolescents are excessively egoistic regarding themselves as the centre of universe and the sole object of interest, and yet at no time in later life are they capable of so much self-sacrifice and devotion. They form the most passionate love relations, only to break them off as abruptly as they began them. On the one hand they throw themselves enthusiastically into the life of community, and on the other hand they have an overpowering longing for solitude. They oscillate between blind submission to some self-chosen leader and defiant rebellion against any and every authority. They are selfish and materially minded and at the same time full of lofty idealism. They are ascetic but will suddenly plunge into instinctual indulgence of the most primitive character. At times their behaviour to other people is rough and inconsiderate, yet they themselves are extremely touchy. Their moods veer between light heated optimism and the blackest pessimism. Sometimes they will work with indefatigable enthusiasm and at the other times they are sluggish and apathetic.[7]

(1)

In this book I have tried to study the adolescent behaviour in the context of American society and the environment in which they are brought up and the effect of the relationships they have with their parents, teachers and other persons. Many young people as they move into the later years of adolescence become aware of the fact that there are many decisions in life which they must make themselves. But there is the pressure to conform, to think as others think. And if they differ from others concerning their beliefs and interests they feel like aliens in the system. They yearn to have a sense of belonging. With this may go a feeling of isolation from others. American adolescents form a population that is hyper-sensitive to counter-cultural ideas and radical suggestions because they look for an escape from the alienation that is caused by the society. They feel rejected by a system that does not give them a meaningful, productive place in society. The process of undergoing socialization in a complex society is enough to cause pain and frustration to the adolescent.

It is against this back-drop that I want to assess the works of Katherine Anne Porter and J.D. Salinger. The first chapter deals with the foremost novelists and short-story writers of America in the twentieth century who have been particularly concerned with the problems of adolescence and maturation.

The adolescent protagonist is one of the most conspicuous aspects of the American novel after the great war. Of course, the trend started at the beginning of the twentieth century with the emergence of "modernism." The war, the social changes, the technological advancement and the new concepts in science and technology—all influenced the entire pattern of life in the West including the arts and literature. "It became common place to talk of modernism in terms of alienation, fragmentation and lack of coherence, centrality, poise or purpose."[8]

Since the aftermath of the great war disintegrated humanity and shattered the old values, new science and philosophy emerged with a new set of morality in respect of sex and spiritual ideals. The new sense of historical crisis and the new social and political forces unleashed in Europe and America such physical, moral, spiritual and psychological strains as burdened man with new responsibility and forced him to recognize new areas of experience. The first chapter is a quick look at such novels of the twentieth century as focus upon the phenomenon of adolescence *vis-a-vis* certain broad changes in American life which have greatly affected the adolescent world.

The second chapter deals especially with the female psyche which underwent many changes due to the rapid changes in the social structure. Because of changing economic conditions, and the decline of the patriarchal family style, there emerged a new emphasis on female equality. With the feminist movement of the 1920s and 1930s, social changes became noticeable concerning the status of the American woman. This chapter focuses primarily on child-adult dichotomy and the double standards for men and women which have been part of the informal religious tradition. The American standard of morality—which has been tinged with Puritan traditions—views an inclination in women towards physical love as the mark of a bad woman. Any strong stirrings within her were things to be ashamed of and had to be strongly suppressed, because "purity, virginity and the joys of the scrubbled feeling which went with chastity were everywhere proclaimed as ideals. In actual practice, however, these things were almost openly mocked at."[9] Thus they observed double standards. The romantic feelings of the women and their femininity was stifled. Their "realization of what they were precluded from enjoying forced them to rationalize their misery by pretending to be immune from passion and desire, while they exhibited their discomfiture and irritation by domineering and scornful attitude and a new rudeness toward man."[10] On the other hand, even in the imaginary world of fiction in the United States, we find the male protagonist trying to escape from bonds of involvement with women and hence the novelists resort to "boyish" themes. Mark Twain's *Huckleberry Finn*, Cooper's *Leather Stocking Tales*, Hemingway's *Nick Adams Stories* and Melville's *Moby Dick* are some examples of stories having adolescent themes. The flight from society is the point of the classic novel, *The Adventures of Huckleberry Finn*, with its concluding sentence: "I reckon I got to light out for the territory ahead of the rest, because Aunt Sally she's going to adopt me and civilize me, and I can't stand it. I been there before."[11]

The nineteenth century saw the gradual emergence of the new woman with her dissatisfaction with her lot, her struggle for recognition, her claim of equality with men, and her emergence from the house into active participation in the social, economic, cultural and political life of the times. All these changes were reflected in the novels of the nineteenth century.

Upto the first World War, there had been a gradual change in the American woman in the United States; but around and after the first World War, due to the number of forces working together, the change was sudden, drastic and overwhelming. The war, its philosophical consequences, the growing industry—all had left no room for Victorian gentility. "The war acted merely as a catalytic agent in this breakdown of the Victorian social structure, and by precipitating our young people into a pattern of mass murder, it released their inhibited violent energies which, after the shooting was over, were turned in both Europe and America to the destruction of an obsolescent nineteenth century society."[12] The generation at that time was actually only disillusioned, shocked, bitter, critical, rebellious, experimental and was ready to overthrow completely the outdated genteel tradition.

The Miranda stories are a brilliant evocation of the childhood of Miranda, who lives in the quick responsive atmosphere of innocence, wrapped round by the safe, happy, sound-enough values of the last of the Southern pioneer aristocrats. Nonetheless, the world of Miranda's childhood is foredoomed by the rapidity of industrial expansion, and we find in "Old Mortality" and "Pale Horse, Pale Rider," how painfully Miranda comes to maturity in the knowledge of her family and of war and of disappointed love. She thus moves between the safe world of illusion and youth and innocence to the hard and actual world of maturity and disillusion and hardwon fortitude.

The third chapter deals with the period of storm and stress which the adolescents are apt to pass through before achieving mature adulthood. Their personality and identity formation is on the way and they are still struggling to find out how others expect them to behave and act. Psychological and emotional stress peculiar to the stage of adolescence may make them feel anxious, in conflict with the family, society, or self; alienated and confused about their role in life. Young people who have grown up with increased expectations about the quality of life and who now face a world of diminishing resources and heightened competition are specially susceptible to frustration, disappointment and cynicism. They may also get alienated in the process. If a person does not adjust and conform to the pattern of society to which he belongs, he/she may get alienated from it.

In literature, drama and arts also, the portrayal of alienation is not new, although its forms have clearly been broadened since the nineteenth-century. The alienated heroes in American fiction and drama, portray some distinctively American responses to finding themselves alienated. Conger explains the concept of alienation as a profound rejection of the values of an adult society that some young people perceive as increasingly impersonal, often cruel and lacking in concern for the individual.[13] Seeman states that alienation refers to a more comprehensive relationship between personality and social system that does deprivation.[14] According to Deutsch,

> The traumatic aspects of adolescence do not leave the adolescents with their dreams of glory; instead some of them go through a period of depressive mood and increased anxiety. Alienated personality has gained great popularity in the recent literature and in the thinking of the general public. Number of alienated personalities seem to be increasing in society and especially in colleges. Let us now forget the general psychological situation in adolescence. The emotional turmoil of this period certainly influences the attitude towards environment. The alienated adolescent proves to be one among many contemporary adolescents: brilliant, gifted, intelligent, outstanding but emotionally empty, lovely, isolated. He/she is from his/her childhood on, limited in his/her acceptance of the values of reality. The alienated suffer not only in the development of the characterological personality, they are also usually neurotically sick.[15]

The adjustment of the alienated persons is difficult at home. Their attitude is different towards both the parents which in turn can affect their adjustment...both the parents are considered as frustrated and dissatisfied.[16] The awareness of the discrepancy between the actual and the possible, may make the adolescence alienated. Part of the struggle for autonomy and independence, that goes on during adolescence, is a questioning of values. Adolescents frequently question the values and practices that their parents have instilled or tried to instill in their children since birth. Sometimes the questioning of parents' values and beliefs comes from observing that parents do not really live upto the abstract moral principles that they have taught their sons and daughters. The reason for so much questioning of beliefs, values and moral behaviour lies in the fact that adolescence is a time of rapid, cognitive, moral as well as physical development. It is seen that adolescents experience conflicts about independence, doubts about sex, confusion about values and uncertainties about self-worth. Ben notes that generational conflicts arise not out of adolescents rejection of parental values but out of disillusionment when they find that their parents do not practice what they have preached.[17]

Failure to develop one's own abilities, potentialities and lack of adequate personal control may make the adolescent feel anxious, distressed, frustrated and confused and thus alienated. All this in turn can affect adversely the personality development of the individual and may interfere with the formulation of proper social attitudes.

As initiation in literature bears only a tangential relationship with the anthropological and sociological initiation; the initiatory processes differ in nature and extend from the anthropological *rites de passage.* The adolescent goes through a physical or emotional trauma which is followed by a gain in knowledge and a loss of innocence. The prominent examples in fiction of the twentieth-century initiates are: Sherwood Anderson's George Willard, Hemingway's Nick Adams, Farrell's Studs Lonigan, Faulkner's Ike McCaslin and Salinger's Holden Caulfield.

J.D. Salinger's *The Catcher in the Rye,* one of the most popular novels of the Fifties and Sixties among the youth, is the story of hypersensitive adolescent, Holden Caulfield. His main trouble is that he does not want to grow up. The adolescent is perplexed and confused by the hypocrisy, complexity and the lack of genuine love in adult society. He flees from the corrupt world of the "phonies" and tries to seek refuge in the world of other genuine beings. His disillusionment with people and society is so intense that the process of initiation results in a nervous breakdown. The basic theme here is that of a mortal hero forced to compromise his integrity with a pragmatic society. What disaffiliates the hero is his peculiar off-centre vision which sensitizes and distorts his vision of truth in a false world. His behaviour is analysed in the context of various psychologists and psychiatrists perceptions.

In most of Salinger's stories, one of the chief motives is to present a conflict between the individual and society with characters trying to move towards a better definition of the self. But for the most part, French is right in saying that Salinger is "concerned with the effects rather the causes of the human predicament."[18] What he is upto in more of a description of inner life than of social life. Holden, the young protagonist of *The Catcher in the Rye,* is presented as representative of adolescence. His problems are shared by all youths, especially American youths.

Many novels of the twenties and thirties, showed its hero in the broad social context, concerned with the young hero as a victim of society and ending in his more or less successful initiation into adulthood. Novels of the forties and fifties on the other hand, were concerned with psychological processes of the protagonist. The wide acceptance of Freud's theories, which stress the influence of childhood and adolescence on later life, has obviously affected the subject-matter of fiction. The changing financial, social and living conditions of modern society have made the adolescent an archetypal figure for the modern literature. The novels of adolescence published in the twenties and thirties and those published in the forties and fifties, indicate their greater emphasis on the need for social reform as at least one answer to the problems of adolescents. These novels also introduce us to the social and psychological circumstances and many other cultural developments which have affected the adolescent experience in the United States.

The widespread popularity of the adolescent hero is an indication that he embodies some of the most significant literary and philosophical values of the present-day. A few writers—notably Wolfe, McCullers, Salinger and Porter—believe the adolescent to be an embodiment of a cultural *animus*.

NOTES AND REFERENCES

1. G. Stanley Hall, *Adolescence: Its Psychology and Its Relations to Physiology, Anthropology, Sociology, Sex, Crime, Religion and Education* Vol. I and II. New York: D. Appleton, 1904.
2. Erik H. Erikson, "Childhood and Society," *Identity: Youth and Crisis*. New York: Norton, 1968.
3. B. McCandless, *Adolescents: Behaviour and Development*. New York: Halt, Rinehart and Winston, 1971.
4. *Ibid.*
5. W.D. Wall, *The Adolescent Child*. London: Methuen, 1952.
6. P. Blos, *On Adolescence: A Psychoanalytic Interpretation* (New York: Free Press of Glencoe, 1962) 204.
7. A. Freud, *The Ego and the Mechanisms of Defense*. New York: International Universities Press, 1936, 149-50.
8. Van Wyck Brooks, *The Writer in America* (New York: Dutton, 1953) 172.
9. Eric John Dingwall, *The American Woman: A Historical Study* (London: Gerald Duckworth & Co. Ltd., 1956) 154-55.
10. *Ibid.* 83-84.
11. Mark Twain, *The Adventures of Huckleberry Finn* (New York: Harper and Brothers, 1948) 405.
12. Horton and Edwards, *Background of American Literary Thought*, 324.
13. J.J. Conger, "Adolescence: Generation under Pressure," *Curacao The Life Cycle Serier Willemstad*, Multimedia Publications, Inc., 1979.
14. Melvin Seeman, "On the meaning of alienation," *American Sociological Review* 24, 1959, 783-91.
15. Helen Deutsch, "Selected Problems of adolescence with special emphasis on group formation." The Monograph series of *Psychoanalytic Study of the Child*, Monograph, No. 3; Hogarth Press and the Institute of Psycho Analysis, 1968.
16. K. Keniston, *The Uncommitted: Alienated Youth in American Society*, New York: Harcourt Brace Jaranovich, 1968.
17. D.J. Ben, "Beliefs, attitudes and human affairs," Belmont, Calif. Wadsworth, 1970.
18. Warren G. French, *J.D. Salinger* (New York: Twayne, 1963).

2

ADOLESCENCE IN AMERICAN FICTION

The concept of adolescence, as generally understood and applied, did not exist before the last two decades of the nineteenth century. The phenomenon of adolescence and its treatment can be related to certain broad changes in American life—above all, to changes in the structure of the family as part of the new urban and industrial order. The transformation of the United States from an agricultural into an urban and industrial society, exerted a profound influence on the structure of American families. "Towards the end of nineteenth century, many writers identified the 'dangers' and 'temptations' which threatened youth directly with urban life. Something of this had been implicit from the beginning, but now it came clearly into the open."[1] The city became the prime source of corrupting influences for the young. Its chaotic social and economic life, its varied population, its frenzied commercial spirit, and its dazzling entertainments were all sharply antagonistic to proper growth towards adulthood. Caught in the midst of so much change and conflict, the adolescent was bound to experience storm and stress. Kenneth Keniston suggested that during the period of transition from childhood to adulthood "youth culture" is likely to develop. "Youth culture" refers to the special way of life characteristic of large groups of young people of approximately the same age. It is not, Keniston writes,

> so obviously transitional...(but is)...more like a waiting period...a temporary stop-over in which one can muster strength from the next harrowing stage of the trip.

Keniston argues that at this age the adolescent is on his own in the formation of an identity. This pattern is characteristic of societies with a high rate of social change and a plurality of alternatives in regard to careers, moral codes, and life styles.[2]

All of this seems to describe nineteenth-century America fairly well, especially the new life of the cities. Social and economic change was everywhere apparent; ambitions were high, there was an astonishing diversity of people, ideologies, occupations. The disparity between generations was assured; it indeed became a part of the national mythology.

The foremost novelists and short-story writers of America in the twentieth century have been particularly concerned with the problems of adolescence and maturation. More often than not, their heroes or protagonists are young boys and girls who go through a *rite de passage*, a multi-faceted growing-up process in a moment of crisis, in which they are suddenly obliged to make the painful transition from childhood to adulthood. This painful transition is known as initiation.

Initiation is essentially a process by which the hero gains self-knowledge and finds his own identity. In the process he also learns about the world he lives in and the nature of evil. If he grows through the process successfully and gets a better knowledge of himself, he learns enough to find a place in society for himself. Thus, the purpose of successful initiation is integration into society.

The theme of initiation is important in American literature for several reasons. In a youth-oriented civilization the theme enables the writer to focus on the crucial period in adolescence when the protagonist makes the transition. The theme also enables the writer to deal with the social forces, either friendly or hostile, that confront the hero in his quest for experience. The confrontation produces feelings of innocence or guilt in the hero, thus enlarging the scope of the fictional work.

The theme of initiation is of particular importance in American literature. As a young nation that went through the pangs of maturation, America embodies the theme in its very history. The birth of the colonies, the formation of the confederation, the growth of self-confidence and a sense of self-identity, the break from the mother country, heralding the birth of the new nation are the various stages in the maturation of the country.

Nathaniel Hawthorne was one of the earliest American authors to write a full-fledged initiation story. In "My Kinsman," Major Molinen Robin, the protagonist, is an adolescent who comes from the rural area in New England prior to the war of revolution. He comes to the city in search of his kinsman and a new way of life. He is introduced to a knowledge of evil in the city and this constitutes his initiation. He painfully moves from the darkness of ignorance to the light of knowledge, from dependence to independence, innocence to awareness, from a simplistic view of life to a complex, multi-faceted awareness of life. Robin is fully initiated when he decides to stand on his own feet rather than go back to his parents in the village or look for aid from his discredited kinsman Major Molinen. Robin's initiation is, no doubt, a very painful one. He comes to the city thinking he is a very shrewd youth, confident that if anything obstructs his quest, he can bludgeon his way through. Very soon, however, he realizes that the world he is going to enter is far too complex for that.

The subject of initiation attracted many writers of the so-called age of realism, too. There is a lot of truth in Hemingway's statement that all modern American literature comes from one book by Mark Twain called *Huckleberry Finn.* Huck is the prototype of the twentieth century initiate. Hemingway's Nick Adams of *In Our Time* and Hold Caulfield of J.D. Salinger's *The Catcher in the Rye* are two prominent examples.

In the intellectual climate of the late nineteenth and early twentieth centuries, America was conducive to the rise of adolescent fiction and the theme of maturation from the second decade of the twentieth century onwards. Loss of innocence—an important part of initiation—became a prominent topic for discussion among thinkers and writers. It is not surprising, therefore, that by the nineteen-twenties, American novelists began to write almost exclusively about loss of innocence, initiation and maturation. So much so that it came to be considered as a particularly American phenomenon. Leslie Fiedler states that America is the only part of the world where the encounter between innocence and guilt can still be recognized and is still a meaningful reality.[3]

Among other important influences that shaped the fiction of adolescence in the twentieth century are literary naturalism, the example of the English novel and the study of psychology. The work of Emile Zola, and particularly that of his American disciple, Stephen Crane [*Maggie: A Girl of the Streets* (1893) and *The Red Badge of Courage* (1895)] and Theodore Dreiser [*Sister Carrie* (1900)] initiated the frank naturalistic description of the struggle of adolescence and the painful passage to maturity in a hostile world. Charles Dickens, the most popular novelist of the Victorian era, and famous for his description of childhood and youth, gave the world a whole range of memorable young heroes and heroines like Oliver Twist, David Coperfield and Little Dorrit. Moreover, the early twentieth-century English novel was moving towards a candid portrayal of adolescence. Samuel Butler's *The Way of All Flesh* (1903) is essentially the story of Earnest Pontifex's growing up. Somerset Maugham's *Of Human Bondage* (1915), is a similar story about the maturation of Phillip Carey. One of the most important books of the twentieth century, James Joyce's *A Portrait of the Artist as a Young Man* (1916) presents the thoughts of a maturing adolescent, Stephen Dedalus. The book moves from the infantile thoughts and language to the sophisticated stream of consciousness of Stephen. Thirdly, with the advent of Freud and Jung, and the study of the human psyche, a new emphasis was placed on the awareness of subconscious motives; on the conflict between reality and the pleasure principle, especially in the adolescent.

Freudian psychology said that the conflicts a child felt would invariably be heightened during adolescence. It made the novelists aware of the process of initiation. Moreover, the famous American psychologist, William James, in *The Principles of Psychology* (1890) and his brother, Henry James, who produced fiction of psychological realism, influenced the writers of the twentieth century. Fredrick J. Hoffman, who has made a study of the influence of French on European and American culture and literature in his *Freudianism and the Literary Mind* tells us that Nietzsche and Dostoevsky, long before Freud, helped to introduce an understanding of the psychological complexity of the human mind.[4]

Jung's significant contribution to the literature of initiation is his theory of the individuation process. Individuation is a psychological process of growing up, the process of discovering those aspects of one's self that make one an individual apart from others. It is a process of recognition and self-awareness: the understanding of one's weaknesses and strengths as one matures. "The meaning and purpose of the process is the realization, in all its aspects, of the personality originally hidden away in the embryonic germplasm; the production and unfolding of the original, potential wholeness."[5] According to Jung, neuroses are caused by a person's failure to confront and accept some archetypal component of his unconscious. It is clear that these studies have helped modern novelists to portray the process of initiation. The studies certainly help the reader to understand the process of initiation and get an insight into the character of the neurotic initiates like Holden Caulfield of J.D. Salinger's, for instance. Initiation, then, is a peculiarly frequent and appropriate phenomenon in American Culture and American Literature. The history of the nation and the tensions in American society and the American character are responsible for it. As in most Western countries, American twentieth century literature has been increasingly one of 'alienation.' In avant-garde fiction, one can trace the gradual disappearance of the qualities of worthiness formerly attributed to the main characters. Even the strongest go down to defeat. The majority are either victims or slobs. Decency may still be a preserve of childhood (Sherwood Anderson's story, *I want to know Why*, J.D. Salinger's *The Catcher in the Rye*), but the adult world is repugnantly gross. On the other hand, American literature has discarded diffidence alongwith reticence.

Gertrude Stein, an astute observer, said of the American soldiers who appeared in France in 1945 that a great change had come over them since the first world war, for they had lost their provinciality, they were sure of themselves as they listened and talked, accustomed to many human types and ways of living. A somewhat similar change perhaps had come over American writers. Van Wyck Brooks opines that the great new twentieth-century citizen army is no less marked in literature than it is in the field. They are rather collectively than individually more mature, even as the nation has been rapidly and obviously coming of age.[6]

It has often been said that the American literature is a literature of boys. Many of the classics have survived as classics for boys, or one might better say that Cooper, Irving, Longfellow, Dana, the author of *Two Years Before the Mast*, have largely survived as writers of classics for adolescents. T.S. Eliot has plausibly found a lack of maturity in Poe that "comes only with the maturing of the man as a whole," and certain it is that, like Mark Twain in quite another way, Poe is pre-eminently a writer for adolescents. There always was something of the boy philosopher in William James, and this was even one of his charms. Sherwood Anderson's adolescent gropings were matched by those of Thomas Wolfe, a writer of genius who never quite grew up. It can very well be said of American literature that it is always beginning again as adolescent. The youthfulness of the American mind, its adventurousness and zest, has been the great gift of America to the older countries.

"The natural role of the twentieth century man is anxiety," says the General in Norman Mailer's *The Naked and the Dead*; and very often this has been repeated in contemporary writing. And how can we characterize this "age of anxiety," in which William Faulkner says, quite simply, "There is only one question, 'When will I be blown up?'" Faulkner continues, "Our tragedy today is a general and universal physical fear so long sustained by now that we can bear it." It is a very perceptive diagnosis. But that people can bear this fear does not change the fact that it plays havoc with their minds, their nerves, their hearts.

This is one of the obvious explanations of many of the elements of the present age, the notes that especially mark the literary mind and what H.G. Wells called the "frightful queerness" that has come into modern life. The highly intuitive Gertrude Stein also said that life today has ceased to be "real" and has become "strange." This strangeness or queerness, whatever its cause, defines the dominant interests and tastes of the day.

The bewilderment, the frustration, the tension that accompany the feeling of queerness and strangeness, are accompanied as well by a widespread tendency to retrospection in every form, the "remembrance of things past." Much of this surely expresses the feeling that the present is intolerable, too painful to be endured or at least to be thought of. The hero of Dos Passos's *Chosen Country* explains this in much the same way as Faulkner does. Proust's great novel *The Waste Land*, Joyce's *Ulysses* and *The Decline of the West* express the mood of world-disintegration, at the same time when Thomas Mann was working on *The Magic Mountain* in which a sanitarium stood for the world. In that pre-war time there were many who could say, with Alfred Hayes in his *Welcome to the Castle,* "Do not ask me what my generation can have faith in or hope for." But at least in their vision of the world the beloved was not "tumbril bait," as the young girl seemed to the old colonel in Hemingway's novel. Nor did youngmen typically feel as so many felt during the world war. What the soldier Wilson says in *The Naked and the Dead*, "Goddam carrion, that's all we are, men, goddam carrion,"—might almost be called a normal feeling at a time whose recurrent refrain was Auden's "Many have perished; more will." In a virtually chronic state of war, regarding which millions lost any clear conception of the whys and wherefores but which kept them nevertheless in a chronic state of tension, how could the present generation look forward for assurance? The world for them was Faulknerian world of violence and terror.

Just as the external consequences of the war overshadowed the years following it, the intense emotions it aroused were not to be quickly allayed. The war fundamentally affected not only the course of modern history externally, but also man's outlook on the world. Alongside this common image of the war as the demise of a long and rich tradition, one must remember the weariness with peace, the verbal militancy and eager welcoming of war, emerging from some pre-war and much early-war literature. These aspects were, however, overlaid by the lasting impression of the mass slaughter and of the disappointments and frustrations which followed.

On the other hand, the South, till the turn of the century had been basically an uncomplex, unvaried and unchanging place. Always simple in its culture and forever complacent about its socio-economic organizations, it had never felt the need for self-analysis. But with the defeat in the civil war the South was rudely shaken out of its deep slumber and made to face reality. It affected the old traditions and patterns of life. Therefore, in order to understand Southern isolation, it is to be seen in the context of its defeat in the civil war from the realization of which it has never really recovered.

As the assumptions and attitudes of the South were changing, the Southern writer of the twentieth century could not ignore the bafflement and complexity of the situation. "Equipped with Grecian thoughts," wrote Ransom in one of his earliest poems "How could I live/ Among my father's folk?"[7]

Katherine Anne Porter represents a vanishing way of southern life. Rural and largely conservative, tragic in its sense of the past, acquainted with bloody defeat and its lingering symbols, struggling still with the guilt of slavery and the stress of industrialization, the South represents a strong regional identity. That identity stands in opposition to the popular assumptions of American culture: progress, egalitarianism, rationalized existence.

In Ms. Porter's fiction her experience becomes our experience. In her fiction, there is no stultifying accumulation of facts but a sense of life, of things coming to life. In a wider sense her stories embrace two important spheres of her experience: the process of growing up, and what Johnson refers to as "the individual within his heritage."[8]

The initiation stories cast light on Porter's unique perception of the consciousness of the female child. She records the pre-puberty consciousness of the female childhood, which reveal almost cyclical range, beginning from the knowledge of the womb and tomb; fusion and sympathy with nature; the female as a sexual object, and the associated sense of guilt and shame. Her later stories record the subtle and elusive states of adolescence and young womanhood.

Reich pointed out how the increasing sexual emancipation of women and their massive war-time participation in industry did lead to an immense increase in stress and to numerous contradictions which would ultimately lead to their greater refusal of conservative customs. The contradiction could often be between a historically accumulated character structure and new social conditions. Thus he wrote of the woman of 1925: "Her character requires, for example, a strictly monogamous sexual life while in the meantime compulsive monogamy has become undermined socially and ideologically, hence her rearguard action in clinging to stifling conditions."[9]

Reich believed in the supreme importance of the social factor. He stressed on many occasions, that the economic dependence of woman and her abuse as a sexual object determined her need for that self-perpetuating evil but nevertheless protective institution of marriage as it also determined her fundamentally conservative character.

The identity of the American writers who established themselves after World War II is collectively as well as individually distinct. These writers begin by dissociating themselves from both the literary and political inheritance of the Thirties, that is from both naturalism and Marxism. The war gives them unflinching clarity, insight into their existence and a provision of things to come. Whatever the illusions they retain after the war, these seem necessary to their survival; whatever technique of literary evasion or assault they invent, further the same end. Survival appears both the secret and paramount obsession of contemporary man. Yet despite the culture of the post-war era, curiosity violent and hedonistic, angry and apathetic, the American writer makes a place for his imagination in it.

The novels of 1940s show an interest in social issues, but they turn away from these issues to find their real centre in moral problems or inward concerns, the inward private being. This shift in emphasis recalls a characteristic tendency of the fiction in the forties. "It casts doubt upon the potential for survival of the democratic culture that had come to us from the humanistic Renaissance and the Enlightenment. It numbed the individual conscience, including nihilism and acquiescence in the loss of human identity. All these consequences of both the pact and the war were to have an effect upon the fiction of the forties."[10] The fiction writers, therefore, were primarily concerned with the survival of the individual identity in a world deprived of all traditional props.

The "New-Fiction" rejects social, political, philosophical ideas as the legitimate subject-matter of fiction. The writers want to create a pure fiction which would be apolitical and asocial in nature. In the words of Chester E. Eisinger, "The safe generalization of new fiction is that it is without loyalties to any order of society and without hope for a different or better order than the one it sees."[11]

Hall's impression of the adolescent dilemma to the modern era is quite pertinent:

> Modern life is hard, and in many respects, increasingly so, on youth. Home, school, church, fail to recognize its nature and needs and, perhaps most of all, its perils. ...Never has youth been exposed to such dangers of both perversion and arrest as in our own land and day. Increasing urban life with its temptations, pre-maturities, sedentary occupations, and passive stimuli just when an active, objective life is most needed, early emancipations and a lessening sense for both duty and discipline, the haste to know all befitting man's estate before its time, the made rush for sudden wealth and the reckless, fashions set by its gilded youth—all these lack some of the regulatives they still have in older lands with more conservative traditions.[12]

Life may be difficult for the youth because he is treated as a child, while he is physically nearly an adult. Consequently, he has an ambiguous position in society. As Dollard says, "In American society, however, these newly acquired abilities are prevented from functioning. Although the individual is physiologically an adult, he is sociologically a child. This period is one of "detachment of the young person from family control and marked dependence upon his age-group before achieving the degree of individual independence in the making of decisions characteristic of adult status. He is expected to conform to the adult restrictions and mores, and yet he is allowed very few of the advantages and privileges which should accrue at maturity."[13]

The adolescent sense of self, with its multiple possibilities, its uncertainties and its self-consciousness has been viewed as the result of a social position in which one is seen, sometimes as adult, sometimes as child. In the marginal-role view, the adolescent's need for independence and fantasies of the future are seen as the desire to "be grown up," his conflicts and instabilities are seen as the conflict between the desire to be grown-up and a role not yet consistent with being grown-up.

This social-role view of adolescence, places the instability of the adolescent self-reflected in the moods and tantrums and dreams of the American teenager against the background of an unquestioned acknowledgment of the stability and reality of the social order the adolescent was to enter. Underneath the hedonism and rebellion of the teenager lay the conformist. Conformity to the peer culture, then was the first theme of the American treatment of the adolescent in the fifties, of August Hollingshead's *Elmtown's Youth*, Games Coleman's *Adolescent Society*, Albert K. Cohen's *Delinquent Boys*. The second theme was that this peer culture was embedded. At a different level than the sociology of the teenager, American literature also presented adolescence as accepting unquestioningly the reality of adult society. Adolescence was presented as an imaginative expansion of the innocence of childhood facing the sordid but unquestionable reality of adult life. From *Huckleberry Finn* to *Catcher in the Rye*, the true American adolescent brought the child's innocence to a new awareness of adult reality, leading to a vision of the phoniness and corruption of the adult world, which was, however, unquestioned in its reality.

But as the century ends and industrial society assumes its characteristic modern shape, the American sense of despair at and revulsion from the norms of adult life seems to increase. Writers as diverse in sensibility, experience and social orientation as Dreiser, Wharton, and Hemingway have created in *Sister Carrie, The House of Mirth,* and *The Sun Also Rises,* works that are remarkably congruent in their protagonists' ultimate response to their world. Hurstwood, disintegrating under the pressures of his confused longings, can find solace only in the rhythmic motion of his rocking chair pulled close to the warmth of the radiator. Similarly, Lily Brat, overcome by her tortuous social battles, seeks a lost primal warmth by imagining herself cradling a baby in her arms as she relapses into a final narcoticized sleep: and Jake Barnes, made impotent by the war, is unable to imagine a way out of that No man's land of lost souls whose wayward pleasures postpone for ever the psychosexual dilemmas of adult life. In one form or another, the regression to childhood serves as an "over-determined" responses to the limitations of social and individual reality confronting these protagonists. So is Holden, praying to the image of his dead brother, fighting to hold onto what he fears most to have lost, struggling through a barren present peopled by Stradlaters and Ackleys who exploit by arrogance. The false pathos of American society turns out to be the real illness from which Holden suffers. His condition of loneliness and longing becomes a mirror of our own predicament.

What Holden shares with, indeed inherits from such classic American prototypes as the New man of Emerson's essays, the narrator of *Walden*, or of "Song of Myself," or of *Adventures of Huckleberry Finn*, is both a way of perceiving reality—a "horizon of expectations," in the words of E.H. Gombrich—and a way of speaking that enforces this view on the reader by discrediting or delimiting all potentially competing voices.[14]

To summarize, all accounts for adolescence stress both the sense of questioning and the parallel discovery or search for a new self of the adolescent. Usually this questioning and search for self has been seen as the product of the adolescent's marginal role between childhood and adulthood.

NOTES AND REFERENCES

1. George H. Hepworth, Rocks and Shoals. Boston: American Unitarian Association, 1870; and Mowry, *op. cit.*
2. Keneth Keniston, "Social Change and Youth in America," *Daedalus* (Winter, 1962) 145-71.
3. Leslie Fielder, "From Redemption to Initiation," *New Leader* (May 26, 1958).

4. Frederick J. Hoffman, *Freudianism and the Literary Mind* (Baton Rouge: Lousiana State UP, 1945) 313-21.
5. C.G. Jung, "The Archetypes of the Collective Unconscious," *The Collected Works of C.G. Jung*. Herbert Read (New York: Pantheon Books, Bollingen Series XX 1966), Vol. VII, 110.
6. Van Wyck Brooks, *The Writer in America* (New York: Dutton, 1953).
7. John Crowe Ransom, "The School," *Poems About God* (New York: Halt, 1919) 172.
8. James William Johnson, "Another Look at Katherine Anne Porter," *Virginia Quarterly Review*, 36 (Autumn, 1960) 602.
9. C.A. Reich. *Character Analysis, op. cit.*, Introduction to 3rd edition, 1948, xxv.
10. Chester E. Eisinger, "Introduction: The Shape of the Forties," *Fiction of the Forties* (Chicago: University of Chicago P, 1963) 3.
11. *Ibid.* 232.
12. G.S. Hall, *Adolescence: Its Psychology and Its Relations to Physiology, Anthropology, Sociology, Sex Crime, Religion and Education*, Vol. I. New York: D. Appleton, 1904, xiv-xvi.
13. John Dollard, Leonard Doub, Neal E. Miller, O.H. Mowrer, and Rober R. Sears, *Frustration and Aggression* (New Haven: Yale UP, 1939) 94.
14. E.H. Gombrich, *Art and Illusion: A Study in the Psychology of Pictorial Representation* (Princeton: Princeton UP, 1960) 60.

3
Adolescence in the Miranda Stories

During the years of rapid physical and social development, the child's identifications are changing as he becomes exposed not only to parents, but to an ever wider array of other significant figures outside the family. The identifications help to provide a child with "some kind of a set of expectations as to what he is going to be when he grows older, and very small children identify with a number of people in a number of respects and establish a kind of hierarchy of expectations that seeks 'verification' in life."[1] As Erikson comments, "The fate of childhood identifications in turn, depends on the child's satisfactory interactions with trustworthy representatives of a meaningful hierarchy of roles as provided by the generations living together in some form of family."[2] The adolescent or adult with a strong sense of ego-identity sees himself as a separate, distinctive individual. In order to have a clear sense of ego-identity, the adolescent also requires a self-perceived consistency not only at a particular moment, but over time. In Erikson's words, "The younger person, in order to experience wholeness, must feel a progressive continuity between that which he has come to be during the long years of childhood and that he promised to become in the anticipated future; between that which he conceives himself to be and that which perceives others to see in him and to expect of him."[3] The reasonable consistency of any developmental influences, contribute to an overall sense of ego-identity. The beginning of the child's ultimate identity are already being shaped during the earlier periods of life, starting with the child's initial orientations of basic trust or mistrust of the people and world around him.

The theme of these stories is the child's growing awareness of the world around him. As the child is innocent, any sudden confrontation of the complexities of life and adult behaviour is bound to confuse him. The impressions he receives from the family and the scenes, put him into a dilemma. As an awareness of the members of his own family is the child's first contact with reality, his first task is often the one of understanding them by discovering the patterns of their behaviour and responses. Because of inexperience the child needs to have some sort of a consistency in the behaviour and responses of the adults in his family. Wherever he notes inconsistencies, he feels that the world as he knows it is crumbling down. A certain degree of consistency of behaviour in his family makes the world predictable to the child and thus helps him bear the actual confusions which are a part of life.

Miranda is exposed to the reality of the adult world at a time when she is too young to understand it. She receives even less help from the adults in her family. The very immensity of the problems she faces forces her to dissociate herself from the adults she needs most. The nature and causes of failure of adults to assist children in their growth are explored in these stories.

For some adolescents changes in their feelings can be very confusing. Their sexuality is one of their most baffling concerns. During this transition period some find it too difficult to adjust to their new feelings about sex. "The conflicting emotions create a storm of feelings deep within the adolescent that cannot be fully resolved until he has expressed them in words and come to understand them. If they remain unresolved, at an unconscious level, they will seek and find some outlet."[4]

The young Miranda is taken to see her first circus. At first she feels comfortable and rather grown up as she is included in the family trip. But soon her response takes the form of traumatic shock. Her first sexual threat comes from two street-wise boys. She cannot understand the sexual meaning of their "look so peculiar." She finds unfriendliness in their grinning stare. And when she asked Dicey about this, Dicey drew her knees together, and warned her to "stop throwing yo' legs around that way." Miranda is confused over the sexual curiosity of the boys against which she has to protect herself, and her initiation into the horrors of the adult world comes immediately.

In "The Grave" too she is made aware of the fact of her sexually being different from her brother. She cannot understand why her dress has to be different from her brother's. The story describes the contemptuous attitude of the country people towards her way of dressing up. Dressed in tomboy fashion, following her brother Paul, she meets along the road some old women. Looking at her they say, "Ain't you ashamed of yourself, Missy? It is against the scriptures to dress like that. Whut yo Pappy thinkin about?"

The rabbit incident of the story shows her awakening sense of her own sexual identity. Paul shoots a rabbit and slits open its body and they find that the animal was about to give birth. The knowledge makes Miranda uneasy. She learns about reproduction of human life, but awareness of this knowledge is a forbidden knowledge and the children feel guilt and shame. "A conspiracy of silence about sex or banal exchange on the level of advertising clinches are still characteristic of the wider society. Such practice prevents young people from clarifying their own attitudes about one of the most forceful drives at this age. It pushes them into clandestine experimentations that often frighten or demean them."[5]

The psychiatrists observe that "The problems of sex should be treated frankly and openly whenever they arise. Sex education should begin when the child is very young and it should be given in small amounts for they can absorb only simple, brief answers. Adolescents need even more to know the social implications of sex."[6] An effort must be made to remove the mysteries of sex and when its role in happy life is explained—we can more reasonably expect the idealistic adolescent to behave in an emotionally healthy way.

In "The Circus" the image of the grown-up dwarf is important. For the first time Miranda's fears are projected into the adult world. The story shows that development is not always growth. Marcus, comparing it to other stories, comments: "Only Ms. Porter's story suggests that the disillusioning experience will have long-range effects and since the suggestion is that they will be damaging, her story raises the possibility that the maturation process in all initiation stories should be further classified according to the proportion or balance between emotional damage and growth which they show."[7]

In "The Circus" Miranda is terrified to see a clown walking high on a thin wire. Her perception of danger and possible destruction terrifies her and she is completely subjugated by her fear. The sensitive Miranda cannot bear the audience's shrieking and laughing "like devils in delicious torment." She screams too, but with real pain. She feels that the crowd's responses are very much different from hers. In "What Is An Initiation Story," Mordecai Marcus refers to the views of Adrean H. Jaffe and Virgil Scott: "Initiation occurs when a character, in the course of the story, learns something that he did not know before, and...what he learns is already known to, shared by, the larger group of the world."[8] At this moment of insecurity when she needs help and protection from the family, she is sent home with Dicey. And the separation at this moment leads to isolation. Her isolation intensifies when she finds all other members of the family enjoying themselves. Utterly frustrated, she feels the world to be too powerful and beyond her control and understanding. "Until adolescents are really confident and independent they like to feel that help and moral support will be forthcoming when needed. This new role for parents and other adults who deal with adolescents is not always easy but it won't be too mysterious or too difficult for them if they accept the fact that young people change, so must adult's roles change."[9] In the story the emphasis is not only on the failure of Miranda's understanding the world, but the adults too fail to realize Miranda's responses. Though the grandmother can understand partially the reactions of little Miranda, she cannot soothe her. She criticizes children watching the circus, but cannot ease Miranda's pain. Her father fails to comprehends Miranda's pain, and does not give her any sense of security. Her sense of alienation increases when she finds all other children enjoying the circus. Finally, she is sent to sleep, and while asleep she sees the terrified faces of the clown falling to his death. She begs Dicey not to turn out the lights and not to be angry with her, but once again the efforts to soothe her turn out to be false and deceptive and the story ends with an unresolved tension, leaving the adolescent alone fighting his fears.

Nance sums up the meaning of the story: "The explicit theme of 'The Circus' is Miranda's initiation into the new dimension of experience and her failure to cope with it satisfactorily because of her mystery of sex in the form of boys looking up through bleachers is also beyond her understanding at that early age. The result of her day at the circus is fear, which in itself is both ordeal and mystery—an initiation process and also a permanent inseparable fact of her life."[10]

The adolescent is distinguished by a purity of moral vision which enables him to perceive or state the moral simplicity hidden by adult complication. He is betrayed, exploited, or neglected by the adult world. His needs may go unrecognized by adults too busy to give him the concern he requires; or as an innocent bystander, he may get in the way of adult corruption and be hurt or destroyed; or he may be direct victim of adult malevolence. "The adolescent passive and powerless in relation to the adult world; his only resource is knowledge, and the strength which may eventually accrue from it. His antitype is the newest and most disturbing representation of the adolescent as victimizer."[11]

One psychiatrist writes that "Disordered feeling or emotion is the basis of all neurotic disturbance."[12] He further adds that "when dealing with an adolescent the most important thing is the establishment of a positive relationship. This involves a transference of the adolescent's childhood attitudes or emotional habits of love and admiration toward his parents.[13] Once this positive relationship is established, the succeeding talks will provide opportunities for giving help in many ways. The adult who is aware of an adolescent's emotional problems early in its development can be very helpful to him. "The fear, the anxiety creates a storm of feeling deep within him that cannot be fully resolved until he has expressed them in words and come to understand them. Whatever can be done to foster this will obviously be of real preventive value."[14]

Some crucial events in Miranda stories articulate how parental authorities to a large extent accelerate the schizophrenic problems. The parental upbringing many a times ingrains unrealistic values, aspirations and roles in feminine life, and incapacitates them to cope either with their own nature or with the harsh realities of adult life.

Miranda is baffled over the way Grandmother and aunt Eliza pick at each other, since in her innocence she had full faith in Grandmother's authority and behaviour:

> Miranda, watching and listening—for everything in the world was strange to her and something she had to know about—saw two old women, who were proud of being grandmothers, who spoke to children always as if they knew best about everything and children new nothing at all and they told children all day long to come here, go there, do this, do not do that, and they were always right and children never were except when they did anything they were told right away without a word. And they were bickering like two little girls at school, or even the way Miranda and her sister Marice bickered and nagged and picked on each other and said things on purpose to hurt each other's feelings. Miranda felt sad and strange and a little frightened. (C.S. 359)

Essentially the self is fragmented in the conflict between social conditioning and natural impulses. The suppression of truth is necessitated by the social structure, and Laing is justified in thinking that in women particularly, it compels a false self so that the authentic one never surfaces; the false self is taken as the normal, the sane and the traditional.[15] The true feelings and the true experiences are condemned and attacked because they do not conform to the role-models formulated by the social hierarchy.

The lies and the betrayals confuse as well as horrify the young mind. In this context, the rabbit-incident in the story "The Grave" is of utmost importance. Miranda's brother instructs her not to tell anybody, as he is afraid that their father will not approve of his "leading (her) into things" like this. It would seem, that she buries down this experience deep in her mind. She "never told, she did not even wish to tell anybody. She thought about the whole worrisome affair with confused unhappiness for a few days. Then it sank quietly into her mind and was heaped over by accumulated thousands of impressions...." "The Grave" is a simple and tremendously powerful little story of two children's contact with the mysteries of life and death.[16] In her ignorance she dreads womanhood, and delivering children. There is a kind of shocked delight. She learns that giving life means risking death, and thus links her femaleness to the bloody ritual of birth. She learns that life is doomed to death. It is subject to corruption and death, and the world is full of chaos, disaster and destruction.

Understanding the secret of her own sexuality, and the taboo accompanying this knowledge, Miranda senses a mysterious threat in her femaleness which will bind her still more closely to the rules of feminine decorum. In spite of the dangers of modern society it would nevertheless seem that parental timidity is the worst possible assurance against girls going astray. James Hemming writes:

> Adolescents are by nature, unless discouraged, thoroughly life-affirming. Effective guidance in sex, therefore, must be the guidance of affirmation. This means that the parent should look forward to their daughter's puberty and be glad when it occurs. They should give her—or see that she knows—all the facts of life, including the emotional facts, and the facts of birth control. They should watch with sympathetic pleasure as their daughter follows the sequence of her maturing emotions...they should encourage her in a positive respect towards herself.[17]

Self-image is another concept which is often seen as being closely related to role development, and a number of writers have contributed to theory by considering this aspect of adolescent personality. For example Rosenburg writes: "At this stage of development—between about fifteen and eighteen years of age—the individual tends to be keenly concerned with his self-image."[18] What am I like? How good am I? What should, or might I become? On what basis shall I judge myself? Many adolescents are consumed with questions of this sort.

"Old Mortality" confirms what the sketches revealed about Miranda and adds new details. An idealistic, romantic, perceptive, and imaginative character has already been established. "Old Mortality" describes how an ideal of femininity is communicated to the young Miranda. She is acutely conscious of her approaching maturity:

> Miranda persisted through her childhood in believing, in spite of her smallness, thinness, her little snubby nose saddled with freckles, her speckled grey eyes and habitual tantrums that by some miracle she would grow into a tall, cream-colored brunette like cousin Isabel; she decided always to wear a trailing white satin gown. (C.S. 176-77)

Miranda wants still more fervently to be like Aunt Amy, beautiful "as an angel," unequalled as horsewoman, lighter and more delicate than any dancer before her time or since, remembered for her quickness of art and her charming ways with men.

According to Rosenburg, the reason for this heightened self-awareness and concern with self-image is that in the first place, adolescence is a time of such major change, both physical and psychological, that faced with pressures of this kind any individual will be forced to re-assess and take stock of himself. Secondly, adolescence, particularly late adolescence, is an age at which may fundamental decisions present themselves.[19]

"The Fig Tree" is another initiation story. Porter herself commented on this story: '"The Fig Tree' is typical of the sketches. It is composed largely of generalized narrative and comments on many aspects of life. Chronologically it would have to be placed not later than 'The Circus' since in it the grandmother is still alive. Miranda's apparent age in the story would seem to place it near 'The Circus' and before 'The Grave,' since the latter story, in which she is nine, indicates a greater understanding of death than does the present one. But it seems more fitting to place 'The Fig Tree' last among sketches, for it forms a balancing contrast with the first and it seems to carry Miranda further than do any of the others toward independence from the family and mature understanding of life."[20]

There is an attempt on the part of Miranda to grapple with the microcosm of life through life and death process. She thinks over the reality and universality of death:

> Dead meant gone away forever. Dying was something that happened all the time, to people and everything else. Somebody died, and there was a long string of carriages going at a slow walk over the rocky ridge of the hill towards the river while the bell tolled and tolled, and that person was never seen again by anybody. (C.S. 354)

In this story too, Miranda is dominated by her grandmother and her curiosity to know things is curbed. She reflects:

> Back into the house she went on tiptoe hoping not to be seen, for Grandmother always asked: 'Where are you going, child? What are you doing? What's that you're carrying? Where did you get it? Who gave you permission?' and after Miranda had explained all that: even if there turned out not to be anything wrong in it, nothing ever seemed so nice any more. (C.S. 355)

The symbolic approach to the story lends a certain depth to the theme of negation which is embodied in the psychological details. Nance compares the two stories "The Grave" and the "The Fig Tree." "There is a parallel between 'The Fig Tree' and 'The Grave,' in the fact that in each story Miranda emerges from a grave into a new phase of development. Her complete emergence from the grave of her grandfather in the first symbolizes her advance from the childhood toward maturity, with its bitter knowledge of death, the final oppressor. In the second, her spirit is released from the grave of ignorance and narrow limitations, just as it is released from the little grave under the fig tree, where it has been imaginatively confined."[21] This story lends Miranda a wider understanding of life and death as well. "The Circus," "The Grave" and "The Fig Tree" have the same dominant theme: theme of initiation into the world of reality, into the mysteries of life and death.

The story 'The Grave' does acknowledge the interdependence of life and death, finally showing the victory of life over death. But it is after twenty years later, in a Mexican market place, "the episode of that far-off day leaped from its burial place before her mind's eye," and there is a surprising difference in her responses. She accepts that in life birth, death, decay are intermixed and she looks towards life positively. Had she got help from her family to understand these things in her childhood, she would not have taken so many years to get rid of the horrors of this experience.

During adolescence, a person is likely to be more concerned about moral values and standards. At the same time, the demands placed upon the adolescents are changing in a great speed, and this in itself requires the need to remain strict to some basic moral values. As Erikson comments, "This is the country of changes; it is obsessed with change." In his words:

> I would...claim that we have almost an instinct of fidelity—meaning that when you reach a certain age you can and must learn to be faithful to some ideological view. Speaking, psychiatrically, without the development of a capacity for fidelity the individual will either have what we call a weak ego, or look for a deviant group to be faithful to.[22]

Only with the onset of adolescence, and the further development of formal operational thought, is the young person likely to reach the post conventional stages of moral development, characterized by "a major thrust toward autonomous principles which have validity and application apart from authority of the groups or person who hold them and apart from the individual's identification with those persons or groups."[23] It is at this point that the adolescent may no longer be able to adopt without question the social or political beliefs of his parents in the happy conviction that solely because his parents have particular beliefs, all right-thinking person must share them.[24]

Preoccupation with the problem of moral values is also likely to be fostered by changing societal demands during the years of adolescence. The average younger child lives in a world that is relatively more homogeneous, more limited than that of the adolescent. As a result, he faces fewer demands for making moral choices. But as he moves further into adolescence, the young person is confronted with an increasingly diverse world in which the necessity for choice are multiplied, "The adolescent who is beginning to look forward to an entire life time is much more in need of a set of guiding moral principles—if his life is to have a semblance of order, consistency and meaning...."[25]

Like Henry James, Miss Porter was determined to obtain "knowledge at the price of finally, utterly 'seeing through' everything."[26] She does not reject or condemn the old order of its inadequacies. She values a stable society, where people share ideas, habits, intuitions and customs. She desires a society in which "there is no groping for motives, no divided faith: people love their past with that uncritical, unquestioning devotion which is beyond logic and above reason. Order and precision they know by heart. Instinctual obedience to changeless laws of nature, strait fidelity to their inner sense mark all they do."[27] She admires Henry James because

> nothing came to supplant or dislocate in anyway his early affections and attachments and admirations. This is not to say he never grew beyond them, nor that he did not live to question them, for he did both; but surely no one ever projected more lovingly and exactly the climate of youth, or budding imagination, the growth of the tender, perceptive mind, the particular freshness and keenness of feeling, the unconscious generosity and warmth of heart of the young brought up in the dangerous illusion of safety; and though no writer ever "grew up" with more sobriety and pure intelligence, still there lay at the back of his mind the memory of a lost paradise; it was in the long run the standard by which he measured the world he learned so thoroughly....[28]

Miss Porter too desired to understand the past and compare it to the failures of modern man in a mechanized, chaotic world. She believed in an ancient system of ethics, unanswerable, undispensable moral law. C.H. Holman writes:

> The South is more distinctive a region than any other section of the United States is. Far more important than its geographical boundaries—than Mason's and Dixon's

> line and the Mississippi—are the boundaries of experience and tradition which have given it a unique identity in the nation. These experiences have taught it attitudes sharply at variance with some of the standard American beliefs; among these attitudes are the sense of failure, which comes from being the only group of Americans who have known military defeat, military occupation, and seemingly unconquerable poverty; the sense of guilt which comes from having been a part of America's classic symbol of injustice, the enslavement and then the segregation of the Negro; the sense of frustration of which comes from the consistent inadequacy of the means at hand to wrestle with the problems to be faced, whether they be poverty, racial intolerance, or the preservation of an historical past rich in tradition.[29]

After the civil war, the region gave way to materialistic progress, followed by moral decay. But the region remained obsessed with the past as no other portion of America has been. For the Southern writers in the 1920's and 1930's the period was an age of protest against certain aspects of the American present which seemed to many to violate the American ideal. All these writers measured the present against the American dream and found it lacking and they revolted against it. The Southerners themselves did not destroy their heritage. Against the ill order of modern industrialism they looked backward for their answers in the past. C. Hugh Holman says:

> They tended to seek in the past a pattern, to evolve a meaning out of large sweeps of history, converting the pattern of event into myth, and uniting the sense of tragic dignity with the irony of comedy. Some like T.S. Stribling and Hamilton Basso, have tried to construct great connected records of social change; others like Erskin Calwell in his early novels, have fashioned laughter into a social weapon; others, like Katherine Anne Porter and Eudora Welty, have used highly refined and almost poetic, brief art forms to state their visions of experience.[30]

Ms. Porter fears that modern industrial progress destroys individuality and results in an empty uniformitarianism, but at the same time, she stresses upon the constant need of exercising the intellect in the face of conflicting myths. In "Old Mortality" the younger generation wants to find their own truths, their own myths, which they can live by. They do not want to accept the given legends which they find conflicting. In their own process of living they want to learn them. Anthropologists have noticed that in societies in which the status of the young is well defined and integrated into the social structure, change and innovation tend to be low; on the other hand, in societies in which youth's roles are uncertain and adult responsibilities and privileges are delayed, there is a predisposition to change, innovate and experiment. The frustration caused by such confusions and delays generates a readiness to respond to new and alien ideas and to try out alternatives to the power structure and the existing institutions.[31] The nature of the social structure thus determines at least in part the degree of youth's activism. Karl Mannheim elucidated the functionality of youth as a potentially deviant population when he described them as not yet committed to the *status quo* and thus more free to push for change and innovation.[32]

The adolescent's impending maturity works several ways at once. He feels himself compelled to move forward a greater degree of independence as he senses that his identity and his self-realization depends on decisive, although perhaps symbolic, gestures of freedom. And even when these inner, existential pressures are not strongly felt, both the family and the community at large will make it plain to the adolescent that he must give up some of the ties to the family. The adolescent's circumstances are riddles with ambivalences. His parents and the community at large want the child to take and master autonomy. Nevertheless, they remain uneasy lest the youngster may lose control altogether and in one rash act may damage his total life chances. These ambivalences are important in giving us a sense of the emotional turmoil of the adolescent experience.

In "Old Mortality" the society is seen through the eyes of an adolescent girl Miranda. She is shown as a very independent girl who keeps defying the family's and the South's code of conduct for a girl. She is bold and there is a powerful rebellious streak in her nature. The first part of the story shows how elders have formed their opinions about certain things, and the second part shows how the adolescent girl Miranda and her sister Maria, see these legends many a times with their own eyes and find them to be different. Ms. Porter seems to prove that the adolescent's way of looking at things is much more vivid.

The source and strength of stories like "Old Mortality" lies in what Stewart call, "Recognition of the kinds, the legendry and the actual...."[33] In "Old Mortality" Ms. Porter's aim is to bring out the tension between the legend and reality. For the grandmother, the uncles and the aunts, "the past is never dead. It is not even past."[34] This sense of the legendry, romantic past is beautifully evoked in the scene when the Grandmother sighs and weeps over the mementoes from the past. Miranda says the old lady "would sit nearly all day beside old trunks, boxes in the lumber rooms, unfolding layers of garments and small keepsakes; she spread them out on sheets on the floor around her, crying over certain things, nearly always the same things, looking again at pictures in velvet cases, unwrapping locks of hair and dried flowers..." (C.S. 175).

Their father Harry is one of the other members of the family, who is captivated by the past. Speaking of Amy's slimness, he says: "There were never any fat women in the family, thank God." But the girls think about Aunt Kezia and Aunt Eliza who were fat. The children cannot understand why those who look at Amy's picture should say that she was much more beautiful than she is seen in the photograph. For Miranda, Amy is soon reduced to "only a ghost in a frame" (C.S. 173). The children cannot accept their view. The problem lies in the fact that the adults make no effort to communicate their memories of the dead in any meaningful way to the children. So, the dead for the children are only in the form of 'photographs, portraits by inept painters who meant earnestly to flatter and the festival garments folded away in dried herbs and camphor' (C.S. 175). Since the girls cannot ignore the myths about the family past, they are 'drawn and held by the mysterious love of the living, who remembered and cherished the dead' (C.S. 176). But all this is very 'disappointing when the little girls tried to fit them to the living beings created in their minds by the breathing words of their elders' (C.S. 175).

The family's pre-occupation with the past and the dead suggests their escapism. They prefer living in the past which can be manipulated at will. They do not have the courage to face the present. The romanticized version of the past is a source of moral confusion for the young. The past is so much imprinted in the minds of the adults that they visualize even the future as a mere repetition. They regard life as something to be 'suffered,' as is clear from the poem written on Amy's grave stone. B.D. Lurch writes:

> If the social norms of the adult group around an adolescent are clear and unconflicting, it is not too difficult for him to make at least a superficial adaptation to these standards, even though they may be narrow. In every generation the vigorous minds will seek to find their own values, rejecting some and selecting others; in rigid societies they will either conceal or break violently forth with their differences. However, when a society is itself in a period of rapid change and has many inconsistencies in its system of values, there is sure to be difficulty for the developing youth in finding either a firm point of departure or a realizable path toward his own goals.[35]

The consequence may be the rejection of the adult world. When the child finds the adult overwhelmed with their past, leaving no scope for the present, his isolation intensifies. "Social ostracism and isolation during early adolescence," writes W.W. Cruze, in *Adolescent Psychology and Development*, "almost invariably leave one with a permanent feeling of social inadequacy." He further writes: "The social isolate is usually an unhappy individual dominated by feelings of unpleasantness."[36]

The family continues to play its role throughout the growing-up years. The continuing impact of the family throughout the adolescent period serves to strengthen the original concepts formed in earlier periods. It is within this setting that all other family issues and problems occur and the solutions are dependent upon the climate of feeling. "The cause of conflict is not a result only of the adolescent years"; writes Ira J. Gordon, "its roots lie in the total family situation and history. However, because of the particular demands of this age-group, conflict becomes a focal factor in the parent-adolescent relationship."[37] Ausubel claims, "The most important single cause of parent-youth conflict is the preservation of parents' attitudes that interfere with the adolescent's greatly expanded need for volitional independence."[38]

David Cooper, the British psychiatrist proclaims that the family has become not simply irrelevant to the needs of the children and adolescents, but a malignant force that acts only to frustrate the fulfilment of these needs. In Cooper's view, today's family imposes "social controls in its children that are patently more than the child's needs to navigate his way through the obstacle race laid down by the extrafamilial agents of the bourgeois state."[39] Furthermore, it frustrates the development of a "free sense of identity" by forcing the individual to perceive himself in terms of predetermined family roles, even in later interactions with other social institutions, and makes him feel incomplete, except as he is "glued together" with others in a continuing family system.[40]

According to Margaret Mead, in earlier and more stable culture eras "in which the elders cannot conceive of change and so can only convey to their descendants this sense of unchanging continuity have been, on the basis of present evidence, characteristic of human societies for millennia." In such cultures, "the child's basic learning was conveyed to him so early, so inarticulately, and so surely, as his elders expressed their sense that this was the way things would be for him because he was the child of their bodies and their spirits, their land and their tradition, particular and specific, that his sense of his own identity and his own destiny were unchallengeable."[41]

Miranda finds no interest in the family gatherings, because there one has to listen to those stories only which have already been repeated many times. She is driven by an impulse stronger than the reasons she can find to justify it. As she listens to her father and Eva speaking of familiar things, she feels stifled.

> Miranda could not hear the stories above the noisy motor, but she felt she knew them well, or stories like them. She knew too many stories like them, she wanted something new of her own. The language was familiar to them, but not to her, not any more. The house, her father had said, was full of cousins, many of them strangers. Would there be any young cousins there, to whom she could talk about things they both knew? She felt a vague distaste for seeing cousins. There were too many of them and her blood rebelled against the ties of blood. She was sick to death of cousins. (PH 86-87)

The questions of blood-ties, being loved or hated confuse Miranda's mind. Because the adolescent period is that threshold of life where all such questions perturb the mind and one needs help from the adult society. "Oh, what is life, she asked herself in desperate seriousness, in those childish unanswerable words, and what shall I do with it? It is something of my own, she thought in a fury of jealous possessiveness, what shall I make of it?" (PH 87). "You don't know anything about it," "You have to find out about it," Miranda said to herself (PH 87-88).

As Robert Penn Warren noted some years ago, Miranda in "Old Mortality" is a quester unsatisfied by any inherited truth. At the end of the story, she has found "a truth that will not be translatable, or finally communicable. But it will be the only truth she can win, and for better or worse she will have to live by it. She must live by her own myth. But she must earn her myth in the process of living."[42] And to find her own truth, she must first demystify the family myth of Aunt Amy and Uncle Gabriel. The family's sense of truth is, in short, romantically transcendent: "Their stories were almost always love stories against a bright blank heavenly blue sky" (C.S. 175). But Miranda is unable to understand the family's sense of truth. Though her mind is doubtful about the family myths, she accepts 'life beyond life' in this world and this double perception is deeply fixed in her mind. But when she meets Gabriel for the first time, she is baffled. Ms. Porter has described the young mind's reaction beautifully. "Maria and Miranda stared, first at him, then at each other. 'Can that be our Uncle Gabriel?' their eyes asked. 'Is that Aunt Amy's handsome romantic beau? Is that the man who wrote the poem about our aunt Amy?' Oh, what did grown up people mean when they talked, anyway?"

Gabriel is an ageing drunkard, bleary-eyed, shambling, coarse-talking. He is fond of the races, cut-off by his grandfather without a penny. He is not only physically a contrast to the family myths, but mentally too. He is morally irresponsible towards his second wife. And his wife Honey makes no effort to hide her distaste towards the visitors for she had been living a life of ignorance being a competitor of dead Amy. The girls also find that Gabriel cannot see the bleeding nose of Lucy, his mare, but is only overjoyed with the fact of victory. Miranda had always cherished a secret wish of becoming a jockey, but her thoughts are shattered on seeing the bloody nose of Lucy, and she says, "That's winning too." The glamour of the race is lost for her. The crowd's cheerings fill disgust in her heart. Once again she fails to understand the ways of the world. She develops distrust in everything she hears from adults. She now wants to experience the things on her own before accepting them.

Presumably objective differences with parents about moral or political values and beliefs may reflect an effort to establish an independent identity of one's own, or to express a deep resentment toward indifferent parents.

> It is often difficult to disentangle the interaction between genuine conflicts and values and the personal dispositions which lead the youngster to use the "conflict of generations" motif in resolving some part of the adolescent crisis; and it is easy to be "bamboozled" by the rhetoric which these conflicts occasion.[43]

Another essential feature of adolescence, as Blos sees it, is regression. It is a common belief within psychoanalytic theory that the main threat to the integrity of the personality in early adolescence is the upsurge of the sexual and aggressive drives which threaten at times to overwhelm the individual. Blos, however, is convinced that the danger to the personality stems not only from the aggressive but equally from the regressive pull. He emphasizes that this is the only period in human development during which regression is an obligatory component of normal maturation. Furthermore, this stage-specific regression is seen as being the cause of much transient maladaptive behaviour, and it accounts for a lot of the emotional turbulence so characteristic of adolescence. The reason for this is "the adolescent has to come into emotional contact with the passions of his infancy and early childhood, in order for them to surrender their original cathexes; only then can the past into conscious and unconscious memories, and then will the forward movement of the libido give youth that unique emotional intensity and power of purpose."[44] Blos provides a number of examples of what he means by ego regression. One that he chooses is the adolescent's idolization of famous people. "Their glorified images constituted and indispensable regulator of the child's narcissistic balance."[45]

In the process of disengagement from early objects who are both loved and hated, another throwback to early modes of behaviour is very much in evidence. From this stems much of the aggression, the negativism, the indifference and the plainly obstructive behaviour. The emotional instability of relationships and the contradictions in thought and feeling reflect the fluctuations between loving and hating, involvement and non-involvement which underlie object relations in the early years of life, and are reactivated once again in adolescence.

In "Old Mortality" Katherin Anne Porter deals with what Johnson refers to as the "individual within his heritage."[46] In Miranda stories we find that there is no more of sentimentalism in love relationships. The second generation of various uncles, aunts and cousins is selfish, sentimental, cruel, critical and romantic. Ms. Porter seems to say that if the family is not directly responsible for the individual's problems, it seldom has the positive role of sorting out these difficulties. Though in "The Fig Tree" aunt Eliza helps Miranda clear her doubts, that is not enough. "Both the social scientists and the general public agree that American society provides the child today with fewer and fewer well-established societal identifications. The presence of an aunt, uncle, cousin or even grandparent residing in the home has a far different meaning to the child today than it did a generation or so ago. Implications of support and guidance has almost disappeared in the United States."[47]

"A background of love and trust is," as Erikson asserts, "fundamental. Without this the child's chances of becoming a reasonably happy, effective, contributing adult, of developing a positive self-image, and a sense of his own identity are seriously impaired, as clinical experience and any number of more systematic investigations make abundantly clear."[48]

Indeed, any number of studies make clear that without strong and unambiguous manifestations of parental love, the child or adolescent has little chance of developing self-esteem or constructive and rewarding relationship with others, and a confident sense of his own identity. Parental hostility, rejection or neglect leads to neurotic disorders, psychophysiological and psychosomatic disturbances and character problems, such as delinquency. Most studies indicate that parental hostility or rejection tends to produce counter-hostility on the part of their children, regardless of how it may be expressed.

If the parents are consistently hostile, unaffectionate, disapproving, critical and distant they seek actively to dominate the child by means of autocratic demands, then the home is full of tensions and conflicts and there is a feeling of resentment. In "Old Order" we are told that the Grandmother's behaviour is very authoritative. "Old Mortality" continues the theme of the young girl's inhibitions by her elders. When she is sent to a Convent school in New Orleans, she finds it run by "dull but good natured nuns." She recalls, "all days and all things in the convent of the child Jesus were dull, in fact" (194). She waited for Saturdays when her father would take her to the races.

The legend of Miranda's Aunt Amy, in "Old Mortality" too describes the tight solidarity of the family which surrounds her. She was a beautiful belle excelling in every feminine grace, but unhappy. Her whole life had been a struggle against confinement and convention, personified in her strict, repressive father, who made life dull and unendurable for her. Her passion for freedom was frustrated every time. This dominating attitudes of the adults is a hindrance in the full, free growth of the child's personality, rather it adds to the pains of growing up. Problems obviously due to neurotic tendencies in the parents—or, at least, due to emotional immaturity—mainly take the form of difficulties created for the adolescent by the need to adjust to fathers or mothers who are authoritarian. The authoritarian parent may cause crisis after crisis until finally the adolescent leaves home, sometimes of his own initiative, and sometimes at his parent's demand.

Miranda too leaves her home, and elopes from the convent. But when she comes back, her father cannot take her back. He turns to cousin Eva. "'It is I who have no place,' thought Miranda. 'Where are my own people and my own time?' She resented, slowly and deeply and in profound silence, the presence of these aliens who lectured and admonished her, who loved her with bitterness and denied her the right to look at the world with her own eyes, who demanded that she accept their version of life and yet could not tell her the truth, not in the smallest thing" (PH 85). In her mind she said, "I hate them both," "I will be free of them, I shall not even remember them." (PH 85-86). "She did not want any more ties with her house, she was going to leave it, and she was not going back to her husband's family either. She would have no more bonds that smothered her in love and hatred. She knew now why she had run away to marriage, and she knew that she was going to run away from marriage, and she was not going to stay in any place, with anyone, that threatened to forbid her making her own discoveries, that said 'No' to her" (PH 87).

It has been repeatedly hypothesized that a conflict-ridden home-background induces teenagers, especially girls to use marriage as an escape. This marriage can be interpreted either as an act of rebellion against parents or as a symptom of confusion. Researches conducted in this field discovered that "girls who marry early have less satisfactory relationships with their parental families."[49] Another study revealed a significant correlation between early marriage and an unhappy home background.[50] Additional research found that "married teenage girls were emotionally less stable and balanced than single girls of the same age.[51] Wendell Johnson feels that after a relatively brief time early in the marriage, the young spouses frequently become deeply disillusioned with what appears to them to be an unsuccessful marriage. Making impossible, unrealistic and ideal demands on life, leads to frustration, which in turn leads to demoralization.[52] The degree of demoralization is usually most severe for the teenager who has used marriage as an escape from home or school. The young escapist soon finds that material relationship, especially in its initial stage, is not at all free of problems.

Miranda's motive in eloping is perfectly clear as well. It is the rejection of oppression from family. Eva is repelled by the news that Miranda has eloped. She tells the girl, "If you had been my child I should have brought you home and spanked you, "Miranda laughs out and replies, "And you must know I should have just gone straight out again, through the nearest window, ...If I went the first time, why not the second?" (PHPR 74).

In the Miranda stories we find the adults are there to question every movement of the children: "Where are you going, child? What are you doing? What is that you're carrying? Where did you get it? Who gave you permission?" (C.S. 355). Ms. Porter seems to condemn the institution of family as a hindrance in the development of an individual. The individual has to struggle hard to maintain his identity. Eva goes to the extent of saying that family is "the root of all human wrongs, and it ought to be wiped from the face of the earth." The system of blood loyalties, the families, the past, the order, all these stand in the development of the adolescent. The youth has no claim before the age. The emphasis is on the struggle of the young and the old. The need is for a new society, changes in social institutions.

But Katherine Anne Porter's attitude to family is dual. As a southern writer, she is particularly conscious of the power of family and community. She is conscious of its irresistible power. In one of her essays she writes: "In any case, the blood-bond, however painful, is the condition of human life in this world, the absolute point of all departure and return" (C.E. 191). But as an extension of the family, community must give the individual a sense of belonging. As in "Maria Conception" even after committing a murder, Maria experiences "...a strange, wakeful, happiness," (C.S. 21) because of the protection she gets from society.

Piaget believes that the parents' child-rearing practices play an important role in the moral development of the child. According to him, parents tend to be authoritarian in their practices, thereby, helping the child's natural tendency toward heteronomy. If instead, they would change their ways and provide conditions for the child to interact with them in a reciprocal fashion, they would increase the likelihood of autonomy taking root. Thus he states, "In order to remove all traces of moral realism, one must place oneself on the child's own level, and give him a feeling of equality by laying stress on one's own obligations and one's own deficiencies.... In this way the child will find himself in the presence, not of a system of commands requiring ritualistic and external obedience, but of a system of social relations such that everyone does his best to obey the same obligations, and does so out of mutual respect."[53] The amount of parents' interest is obviously a crucial factor in the child's progress toward independence. If parents are too deeply tied to a child, if they bear a love for him so intense that it amounts to dependency, the child's way to autonomy will be blocked. On the other hand, a child who is loved too little, is not provided an easy start toward independence. Here, as in so may areas of parents' behaviour, it is moderation that seems to hold the key to normal growth.

Miranda is perceptive enough to see that Eva's analysis of the 'legend' is every bit romantic. At the end Miranda is beginning her own pursuit of truth and asking herself: "Where do my loyalties lie? Where should they lie?" After her visit to Gabriel's funeral, Miranda says:

> Ah, but there is my own life to come yet, she thought, my own life now and beyond, I don't want any promises, I won't have any false hopes, I won't be romantic about myself. I can't live in their world any longer, she told herself, listening to the voices (of her father and aunt Eva). Let them tell their stories to each other. Let them go

> on explaining how things happened. I don't care. Atleast, I can know the truth about what happens to me, she assured herself silently, making a promise to herself, in her hopefulness, her ignorance. (C.S. 221)

She thus, rejects the old, painful structure, the Judeo-Christian concept of life and death and after-life. She is left along with the griefs of old mortality. As Warren has pointed out, the last five words of the story, "in her hopefulness, her ignorance" suggest one set of assumptions that the past can be "repudiated" in favour of absolute truth in the person. Truth is a concept which is not absolute, but "inheres in the dialectical of the life-process."[54] In this story Ms. Porter raises the question "Where is this new generation of the South which is sceptic about the legend of the Old South, headed to?" There is no definite answer provided to this.

The end of the story shows that Miranda has assured herself that she "does not care" about her family and myths and hopes to find "truth about what happens to her." She realizes that she can find the truth outside the family only, so she rejects all family myth and religion.

"Old Mortality" ends in isolation and desolation: it concludes with a statement bringing together the incidents and making clear the symbols of isolation. Miranda's final thoughts are: "I don't want any promises, I won't have false hopes, I won't be romantic about myself: I can't live in their world any longer, she told herself, listening to the voices back of her. Let them tell their stories to each other. Let them go on explaining how things happened."

Keniston observes that alienation implies lack of commitment to the values of society. For example, many have become alienated from what they view as the hollowness and hypocrisy of many conventional social relationships. Those who react by withdrawing into apathy and indifference are in a very different position from those who have attempted to find new and meaningful substitutes,

> Alienation can be expressed in many ways. In one sense the revolutionary and the psychotic are both highly alienated from the norms and values of their society—both reject these norms and values, yet there is a vast

> difference in the way their rejection is expressed: the revolutionary actively attempts to transform his society; the psychotic has undergone a regressive self-transformation that leaves his society unaffected.[55]

The most prominently emphasized alienation currently involves an "explicit rejection of traditional American Culture." Some young persons may respond to their alienation by withdrawing from society as a whole. For some, this may involve deep despair, apathy or defeat, without any meaningful substitute to take the place of their alienations. Feuer cites Plato's view that the generational struggle constitutes the primary mechanism in social change, and Aristotle's assertion that political revolutions are caused "not only by the conflict of rich and poor, but by the struggle between sons and fathers."[56]

Young people often rebel against the reality in which they find themselves and nearly all of them are sooner or later tempted to resent their primary family environment. They almost immediately want to replace it with another form of social reality. Karl Mannheim noted that "dissociation from one's previous reality and the seeking of distance from the primary environment are the principal impulses. It is with a sense of liberation that the adolescent discovers alternative interpretations and new values. Self-assertion and defiance accompany this experience."[57]

Usually the normal adolescent combines a healthy interest in himself with an objective approach. That is he wants to know all he can about his abilities, his position, his prospects and his personality. He constantly questions the values by which he has been brought up, not necessarily with the idea of abandoning them but rather of examining their usefulness to himself and his generation. As a consequence a strong societal demands for independence, in the face of incompatible and well-established dependent responses, the adolescent is, not surprisingly, likely to be in conflict. And the fact that this conflict is timed to coincide with so many other developmental demands related to puberty and adolescence only tends to increase its stressfulness. Furthermore, today's adolescents often find inconsistencies in the way people react to them as individuals. Needless to say, such contradictory expectations can be a significant source of conflict and anxiety for the adolescent. But not all problems of achieving independence stem from inconsistencies on the part of society or parents. The adolescent himself is in a state of conflict. He may desire to be independent, but at the same time he may want security which is associated with dependence.

R. Nixon believes that the adolescent, "is normally uncertain, anxious, oversensitive and a little apprehensive. Much adolescent behaviour is the normal result of normal growth. But the parents need to remember that they passed through this period and to realize that they need to develop a better understanding of normal adolescence."[58] The recent and continuing changes in the nature of the family and its relation to society, and the rate of those changes have certainly increased the stress on today's nuclear family. Social fragmentations and disorganization increased the difficulties of the adolescent period.

Since World War I, many happenings have changed the tenor of adolescence in America. Vehement uprisings of restless youth have shaken American society. Primarily because of changing economic conditions, the patriarchal family style declined, and there emerged a new emphasis on female equality. With the feminist movement of the 1920s and 1930s, social changes became noticeable concerning the status of the American woman. No longer rigidly controlled by the family, she spent a great deal of time in institutions that helped her to unfold her talents. There was a general shift in the perception of the institutions of marriage and the family. These primary institutions were formerly viewed as sacred, inviolable arrangements to which people must adjust. The secular philosophy and attitude, in contrast, saw such institutions as arrangements that should be changed when human needs and desires call for such changes. The young woman's decision concerning marriage became individual rather than a family enterprise.

With the decline of family system correlated with the rise of secularism, the focus of concern shifted from the family to the individual. Modern American life granted to both males and females the right to seek personal pleasure and satisfaction without the impediment of control by the parental family. This social change was greatly relevant to the female who, for example, could now easily obtain a divorce if she felt that her personal needs, sexual and otherwise, were not fulfilled in a given marriage.

The new and traditional forces confuse the adolescent mind. With the modern emphasis on individuality and personal decision-making, the adolescent is left largely on his or her own to work out a suitable blueprint. Professor Winston Ehramann called it the "great sex dilemma"[59] of the 1930s. Youth was caught between two opposing forces that exerted nearly equal compulsion. In the twentieth century, sexual liberation made giant strides and progressively weakened traditional sexual mores. Though the cultural heritage of American society includes principles of the Judeo-Christian tradition, which forbid premarital sexual relationships, yet these principles are giving way to more secular views. When Ms. Porter was writing, a girl's chastity was of immense importance. For the woman, sex was expected to be of little or no personal interest.

Ms. Porter has strongly condemned these double standards which are especially biased against the female. From the Grandmother, Sophia Jane to Miranda, Laura, and Violetta she has very powerfully depicted the innermost feelings of the female and the outcome of the suppressed feelings.

The sketches in "The Old Order" make significant observations about the life of those days in the South by probing deeply into the heroine's mind and spirit. "The Journey" might be examined as a feminine statement, in the sense that it not only traces the roots of Grandmother and Nannie but also the roots of the oppression and victimization of women. The Grandmother, Sophia Jane, fantasizes that as a maiden "She had lost her virginity, her claim to regard, even to existences, and after frightful moral suffering which marked altogether her physical experience, she would wake in cold sweat, disordered and terrified" (235). Her fears reveal her fear of the male-prescribed values. William L. Nance sums up his views about female chastity: "The concentrated description of the inner life of a young girl of the old order indicates some of the ways in which her training distorted her developing instincts and helped prepare for a life of frustration: the absolute value placed on 'virtue,' irrecoverable once lost, by the code of Southern purity (for women); the air of mystery and evil, and the consequent fear and guilt, which resulted from the complete parental silence about sex; the sentimentalizing and falsifying of emotion caused by its forceful separation from reality."[60]

The double standard in sexual relationship could result in guilt feelings. Whereas a man could find sexual gratification outside the marital bond and still retain his self-respect, any personal sexual gratification on the part of the wife could lead to her bad reputation. In Christianity's view, sex before or outside of matrimony was sinful for both sexes, but far more sinful for women. If a woman was discovered by a Puritan community to have indulged in premarital coitus, a public confession had to be made before the entire congregation.[61]

One of the most notorious confusions within the blueprint of the American society concerns sex. On the one side, sex and "love" are glorified and, on the other side, there ensues a furtive and guilt-ridden apprehension when questions are raised concerning the facts and specific activities of sex. The inconsistent polar concepts cause confusion and anxiety among adolescents, who are in the process of trying to arrive at a consistent blueprint for sexual behaviour. The lack of behavioural directives may be of more serious and destructive consequence, to both the personality and to the social system, than the existence of inappropriate and overly stringent views.

"Flowering Judas," where Miranda is named Laura, has been made a compelling story because of the intricacy of the protagonist's simultaneously conflicting and contradictory impulses and instincts. When the story opens Braggioni, the embodiment of all the forces of corruption, comes to Laura's apartment to discover, if possible: whether it would be worth the effort to attempt an assault upon her "notorious virginity." Braggioni's worldliness and his coarse sexuality offend her romanticism. The complex symbolic associations also reveal her impulse of withdrawal.

She is hostile against "violence, mutilation, a shocking death" (93); and sexual intercourse represents to her a violation of both body and soul. She gives up the thought of marriage and chooses to be "a lay nun." Her sense of self is associated with her problem of sexuality. It is only in the dream-state that she can express her desire and need for Eugenio. The images of sexuality reveal that, to Laura, Eugenio embodies her hunger for both spiritual and sexual nourishment.

J.E. Hardy's analysis of the dream casts light on the meaning of the dream: "The dream makes it clear that Eugenio had been trying to seduce her, and she had evidently felt strongly attracted to him."[62] The story obviously depicts the attitudes of non-involvement, and isolation that inhibit the protagonist to establish normal human relationships.

Dorothy S. Redden in her very perceptive article on the story defines Laura's dilemma:

> That she fears death, even that she finds it evil; may be considered unexceptionable, at least in our civilization. An important part of her, however, feels the same way about life, and especially about its vital component of human relationships. To this part of Laura, life is not only a stifling emotional tyranny of love and sex, but a kind of death, equally vicious and sinister, equally terrifying.... Although she goes on living, she fears and hates life. At the same time, although she is drifting toward it, she fears and hates death.[63]

In *The Days Before,* Ms. Porter writes "My whole attempt has been to discover and understand human motives, human feelings, to make a distillation of what human relations and experiences my mind has been able to absorb."[64] There is a stronger instinct to preserve an independent individuality. "Maria conception" deals with a young woman caught in oppressive and constricting circumstances. "Virgin Violeta" is the dramatization of the same conflict in the circumstances that described how the biopolarity of the surroundings (social, religious, cultural) create a cleavage in the psychic corridors of the female child, which she finds unable to bridge. From 'Maria Conception' we move on to the state of rupture in the adolescent female psyche in "Virgin Violeta." The story is the depiction of female puberty: the period of emotional confusion and trauma. "Virgin Violeta" provide us an insight into the fancies, and dreams of a vulnerable girl, torn between the romantic dream of love and her instinctual desire for freedom. At the commencement, she is taught chastity, modesty and obedience. She cannot overcome her confusion because of the disparity between the standards of the outside world and her inner thoughts. As an adolescent she is day-dreaming, shy and erratic. Her romantic dreams contrast with the real behaviour of physical world. So the sense of oppression is inevitable. This sense of oppression is visible in her world in symbols: "as the gaily coloured parrots in the markets, stuffed into tiny wicker cages...gasping, panting, waiting for someone to rescue them" (26). The story reveals the motives of repression and guilt as an adolescent girls's response to the established codes of chastity and modesty.

Most American critics point to the 'psychological' aspect of Ms. Porter's work. Her fiction reveals insightful and learned observations on feminine psychology. In her commentary on Katherine Mansfield, Porter writes: "With fine objectivity, she bears a moment of experience, real experience in the life of some human being, she avoids stating any belief, gives no motives, airs no theories, but simply presents to the readers a situation, a place, a character, and there it is. The emotional content is present as implicitly as the wheat in the grain."[65]

The First World War served to reveal new depths of human depravity in a world that men had come to think of as civilized. After those four catastrophic years it was difficult to believe that mankind was steadily progressing toward higher and higher stages of civilization. In an influential book, *The Modern Temper* (1929), Joseph Wood Krutch pointed out that man no longer lived in an atmospheric world of stable values. The scientists, he charged, had robbed man of his belief in the beneficence of the universe, and the psychologists had taken from him the sense of his own dignity. There appeared to be no longer any place in literature for heroes like Ulysses and William Tell or for great tragic figures like Agamennon or King Lear.

In the preface to the book *Civilization in the United States* (1922) Harold Stearns describes the World War I years as a period of the failure of culture, entertainment, family life, religion—of everything but science. Bounded as it was by a war and a depression, it acquired an isolated position in cultural history. Certain writers presented World War I as a culminating test of man's loyalties and his moral responsibility. Danger, violence, battle, chaos, death were in every case dissociated from both geography and culture. The post-war American was almost abnormally sensitive to a form of experience that may best be described by the term "violation," a term that indicates what happened to their sense of dignity and security as the result of events that had little or nothing to do with them. That sense of violations present in each of the principal works of American war-literature. Among the forms taken by the feeling of outrage, three reactions are prominent in the war literature of the 1920's: the war as a monstrous hoax, an unendurable outrage committed by the elders, who were brutal, insensitive and stupid; the war as violent re-education of the soldier in the ugliness and the scatological realities underlying the surface of decorum; and finally, the war as a means of testing the true nature of men and of reclassifying them morally.

In the period between the two world wars, or since about 1910, a kind of cultural awakening took place in the literature of the United States. Earlier the writers were chiefly of English stock and were predominantly rural and agrarian in their feeling, and now the writers wrote usually against a background of industry and the city. Maxwell Geismar writes, "With the emphasis on a satiric rather than a tragic America in the twenties, both strains of the Realistic Movement flowed along concomitantly. In John Dos Passos' famous novel—the trilogy called U.S.A.—and in William Faulkner's lurid dramas of the deep South, there were the fused elements of a deep moral conviction as to human justice and of a sharp satiric survey of American society."[66]

Cleanth Brooks wrote in 1971 that Porter's stories and essays reveal a wide streak of the feminist. In her fiction the central experiences are expressed through female characters—what it meant to a woman to say I have a particular body, I live, I feel, I suffer.[67] Porter's literature acknowledges the strong female response to various sociological and psychological conditions, which female consciousness has undergone since primordial times. It seems to reinforce Henry Adams' view: "The study of history is useful to the historian by teaching him his ignorance of women. The woman who is known only through a man is known wrong."[68] Porter had, from childhood, a fierce curiosity about who she was and what her feminine identity meant. Most of her stories, which have women protagonists, are autobiographical. Rober Penn Warren observed "that her heroines search for identity and independence."[69] In her early stories, written and published in the twenties and thirties women are in conflict with themselves or with socially imposed rules. The stories written in the period 1929-30 reveal a level of psychological conflict treated with more complexity and personal intensity. The projection of subconscious mental states: dream, desire and memories, the incisive penetration into the layers of human psyche, combined with present tense realism, characterize these stories. The early stories of *Miranda Stories* describe a young female child's confrontation with the adult world, the mysteries of womb and tomb—the mysterious seats of life and death respectively. There is also an awareness of the implication of human sexuality; love, violence, powerlessness, shock, disillusionment and estrangement. The later collection of *Miranda Stories*—"Old Mortality" and "Pale Horse, Pale Rider"—reveal the disparity between appearance and reality, the pressures of the circumstances and the state of no choice. "Old Mortality" describes Miranda's familiar and social surroundings. She responds to her surroundings; experiences many facets of life and finally in "Pale Horse, Pale Rider," takes her own decisions. "Pale Horse, Pale Rider" is different from the other Miranda Stories because it is imbued with a peculiar atmosphere which permeated the United States during World War I with its perverse sense of patriotism, its distorted vision of the enemy, its sometimes brutal pressures for conformity. The war not only annihilated and corrupted humanity but encouraged sentimental patriotism. The story describes a different area of feminine experience: conflict in love, the death of her lover and final loneliness.

In fact, "Pale Horse, Pale Rider" represents an ultimate in how Katherine Anne Porter could represent the particular dramatized in terms of the general. Ms. Porter gives a completely subjective treatment to time within her heroine's consciousness, symbolizing Miranda's determination to remain loyal to her own convictions. She cannot accept the legend in terms of the older generation. She must find her own terms. In "Pale Horse, Pale Rider," Miranda finds herself as much in conflict with the prevailing values as with any of the past. American culture contains enough child-adult dichotomies to exert a strain on both the interpersonal process and the individual personality. The main impact of this situation is felt by the young individuals at the time when they find themselves between the two relatively well-defined roles. They experience feelings of frustration or they face the problem of readjusting to new positions in the authority pattern.

In "Pale Horse, Pale Rider" the time is 1918, near the end of World War I, when Miranda is working in a newspaper office. She is totally disenchanted with the job because she lacks emotional toughness. The adjustment problems of young people coming to the urban areas, especially of the females coming from traditional families, are relatively timeless and still exist in the United States. The following statement made in 1910, could be easily applied today.

> Never before in civilization have such numbers of young girls been suddenly released from the protection of the home and permitted to walk unattended upon city streets and to work under alien roofs: for the first time they are being prized more for their labor power than for their innocence, their tender beauty, their ephemeral gaiety....[70]

Miranda is perturbed over the perverse sense of patriotism. She is being constantly badgered by Liberty Bond salesmen to give five of eighteen dollars of her small salary. Her boss on the newspaper, is a loving caricature, "exactly like city editors in the moving pictures, even to the chewed cigar." Her friend Chuck Rouncivale, trying to console her after the depressing interview with the broken actor, advises her to "toughen up."

> Forget that fellow.... All you have to do is play up the headliners, and you needn't even mention the also rans. Try to keep in mind that Rypinsky has got show business cornered in this town; please Rypinsky and you'll please the advertising department, please them and you'll get a raise (C.S. 198).

The world for her in nightmarish. Behind all these things looms the war itself. The key to many scenes is found in Miranda's thoughts at the theatre: "We dare not say a word to each other of our desperation, we are speechless animals letting ourselves be destroyed, and why? Does anybody here believe the things we say to each other?" (291).

Adam and Miranda discuss the effects of war. Miranda observes that "the worst of war is the fear and suspicion and the awful expression in all the eyes you meet.... As if they had pulled down the shutters over their minds and their hearts and were peering out at you, ready to leap if you made one gesture or say one word they do not understand instantly. It frightens me; I live in fear too, and no one should have to live in fear" (294). Miranda jokingly suggest to Adam that they run away. But they know that their attempt to make a saner life away from the war will be doomed; they will be trapped by society and their escape into love will be no escape, for death will always be waiting, in or out of the war.

The story mostly represents the response of civilians—as befits a war that was essentially fought by civilians who had temporarily been turned into soldiers. Miranda wanted to run away with Adam, but could not even express her feelings to him, she could not say, "Adam, come out of your dream and listen to me, I have pains in my chest and my head and my heart and they're real. I am in pain all over and you are in such danger as I can't bear to think about, and why can we not save each other?" (296).

Ms. Porter has beautifully described the helplessness of the young lovers in a society ruled by power-hungry adults. Her rage against war could be identified as a distinctly feminine response to war, which Virginia Woolf emphatically articulated: "I would say (war) was stupid and violent and hateful and idiotic and trifling and ignoble and mean display. I would say I am bored to death by war books. I detest the masculine point of view. I am bored by his heroism, virtue and honour."[71]

But it was impossible to recapture the pre-war mood or free the current mood from the images of the fighting and the dead. Even for the noncombatants the mood was of futility. The shrugging of shoulders over the questions of moral imperative, were in large part a consequence of the war. The post-war generation felt honestly that it had been victimized by a gross and stupid deception. Nothing genuine had come out of the war. The elders had made fools of themselves, had involved the young in murderous folly; how could they respect them? The young generation felt their only responsibility was to themselves. In much of the literature of the twenties there was a continuous statement of rejection; this was in part a naive awakening to the existence of new forms of evil in the world, but it also served as an indignant protest against a civilization that had played a bad joke on itself. "As for the faith lost by the intellectuals, there is room to wonder what sort it was to continue serene from 1900 to 1914, and then so suddenly give way," said Gilbert Seldes.[72] The really creative forces of the last one hundred years had been defeated in the last ten.

The memory of the war haunts the fiction of the 1920's. The most important consequence of a traumatic shock is that the experience that caused it is recalled again and again. It is not that victim enjoys the experience and so wishes it repeated, but rather that initially it has thrown him entirely off balance and he is therefore unable to adjust to it.[73]

The shock often has some effects: for one it may upset his confidence in the past—his own past and the social past of which he has been a part. The experience is itself almost equivalent to death; what follows it amounts to a new and a different life. The man who survives violence is often quite remarkably different from the man who has never experienced it. Anger, fear, helplessness etc. are a part of the reaction.

In "Pale Horse, Pale Rider," war and disease destroy Miranda's chances of happiness. There is a concrete encounter with death. Miranda cannot help feeling that existence is death—or, at least, not life. The soul's life is the body's death and the body's life is the soul's death. Here Miranda loses her "hopefulness" as well as her "ignorance." The war is examined in its psychological and moral implications. In the Adam-Miranda relationship war presents the conflict of the individual's obligation to society and to himself. Adam is symbolic of sanity and purity and he represents the American dream.

The childhood sense of fear and oppression blends with the present sense of war, death, loss and despair. In her dream, Miranda sees Adam being repeatedly struck by flights of arrow. Each time he is struck down, he rises again unwounded and alive. She tries to save him by arrows into her own body. But this time they pass through her and kill Adam. Hardy interprets this dream in depth and comments: "The familiar symbolic association of death with the experience of sexual climax—such an association embodied in the commonplace ambiguity of this word 'die' in Elizabethan poetry—is involved here. Miranda wants to die with Adam in the erotic sense, but her dreams express her fear that one or both of them will actually die before their love can be consummated."[74]

Miranda thinks of Adam as a "sacrificial lamb" (295) being sent out to slaughter by older men who jealously want the younger ones dead. "The tom-cats try to eat the little tom-kittens you, know", she tells him (294). In the larger sense, too, Adam and the other young soldiers are the human sacrifices the community is willing to pay to ensure its own security and survival.

Death is a major crisis because it affects the living: the person approaching death, the person close to someone who is dying and the person who is trying to adjust to life after the death of a loved one. While death might be inevitable it involves many uncertainties and has a temporary unpredictable character. For some, death is too terrible to contemplate. For most, it involves a transition from a state of relative security to the insecurity and uncertainty of the unknown.

Ms. Porter shows her rage against the fact that the common man is denied his right to live. There is a wish to live in spite of the odd circumstances. In Miranda's dream too, there is an indication that she does not want to die. She reveals a will to live: "...and there remained of her only a burning particle of being that knew itself along, that...set itself unaided to resist destruction, to survive and be with its own madness of being.... Trust me the hard unwinking angry point of light said, Trust me, I stay" (311).

Miranda in her dream, thinks of the horses she might ride in a race with death. The image of her grandmother appears, spurring her horses forward. She finds a stranger riding easily beside her, and passing her by. She shouts: "I'm not going with you this time—ride on" (270). This dream symbolizes the tragic meeting and parting suggesting the fate of Miranda. Even in these odd circumstances, Adam and Miranda find togetherness. But love has made them more vulnerable. The devastation, the emotional and spiritual sterility caused by war is pervading everywhere.

In "Pale Horse, Pale Rider," Miranda and Adam 'dig in' in spiritual self-defence against the hysteria of 1914 war. The choice is between reality and illusion and the reality is harder to bear. Miranda might dream of a beautiful "nothing" but she must awaken each day to face the ugliness of modernity. In "Pale Horse, Pale Rider," the modern existence is described as detached from the past, the mythical and the sacred circumscribed by suffering and death. There is war and epidemic in the air, yet she desires salvation.

Miranda has a "bitter desire" to disclose her love to Adam. She longs to see him once again, though war and death have taken him away, coming to life again, Miranda hears bells, horns, and whistles mingling. The war too, is over now, but now she does not want life. She assures herself:

> That was a child's dream of the heavenly meadow, the vision of repose that comes to a tired body in sleep, she thought, but I have seen it when I did not know it was a dream. Closing her eyes she would rest for a moment remembering that bliss which had repaid all the pain of

> the journey to reach it; opening them again she saw with a new anguish, the dull world to which she was condemned...." (P.H. 94)

Miranda has to wake up from her sleep. And certainly, she is no longer as naive or as ignorant as she was when she promised herself independence in 1912. She fights the greatest adversary of all, her way to heroism, but now the substance of life itself seems disappointing, and at night she weeps "silently, shamelessly, in pity for herself and her lost rapture." Then she wishes Adam was with her:

> At once he was there beside her, invisibly but urgently present, a ghost but more alive than she was, the last intolerable cheat of her heart; for knowing it was false she still clung to the lie, the unpardonable lie of her bitter desire. She said, "I love you," and stood up trembling, trying by mere act of her will to bring him to sight before her. If I could call you up from the grave I would, she said, If I could see your ghost I would say I believe.... "I believe," she said aloud, "Oh, let me see you once more."

The disaster here is represented by the huge public forces, war and disease, which invade and destroy the private right to happiness. She questions these impersonal forces, but finally she cannot help feeling that existence is death—or, at least, not life. In the end she realizes that she must live by sheer personal integrity and face the pitiless clarity of day-to-day life. She leads a joyless life, threatened and insecure, armed only with her fortitude to face the emptiness of life. The physical and spiritual harrowing leave her with little chance of happiness. Her loneliness is conveyed in the final, ironic lines of "Pale Horse, Pale Rider."

> No more war, no more plague, only the dazed silence that follows the ceasing of the heavy guns; noiseless houses with the shades drawn, empty streets, the dead cold light of tomorrow. Now there would be time for everything.

For Ms. Porter the world is a chaotic place and the chaos is both external and internal. The search for some kind of security within leads her characters to seek love. Robert H. Grinder observes that the adolescent needs to find a sense of identity and a sense of assurance. And finally, he searches for ways to realize his independence socially, emotionally, financially, and intellectually changing from his childhood dependency on adults.[75]

In short, the sense of identity grows, develops, changes as an individual passes from one age level to another. It responds to basic needs and in turn may itself supply both motivations and goals. It integrates drives and responses into patterns that are satisfactory for its growth. When it is threatened, it protects itself from danger by patterns of escape. Though they differ in the type of escape or resolution from conflict, Mitchell writes that what they share is the necessity to reconcile their own needs with the demands of society.[76]

NOTES AND REFERENCES

1. E.H. Erikson, *Identity: Youth and Crisis* (New York: Norton, 1968) 159.
2. *Ibid.*
3. E.H. Erikson, "The problem of ego identity," *Journal of the American Psychoanalytic Association*, 1956, 4, 56-121.
4. Luella Cole, *Psychology of Adolescence*, 7th ed. (New York: Rinehart and Co., 1959).
5. Gisela Konopka, "Requirements for Healthy Developments of Adolescent Youth," in *Readings in Adolescent Psychology*, Cottle, 46.
6. J. Roswell Gallagher and Herbert, *Emotional Problems of Adolescents* (New York: OUP, 1976) 30.
7. Mordecai Marcus, "What is an Initiation Story"? *Critical Approaches to Fiction*, ed. Shiv K. Kumar and Keith Mackean (New York: McGraw, 1968) 205.
8. *Ibid.* 206.
9. Gallagher and Harris, *Emotional Problems of Adolescents* (New York: OUP, 1976) 12.
10. William Nance, *The Art of Rejection* (Chapel Hill: University of North Carolina P, 1964) 87.
11. E.A. Dovvan & J. Adelson, *The Adolescent Experience* (New York: Wiley, 1966) 80.
12. Gallagher and Harris, *Emotional Problems of Adolescents* (New York: OUP, 1976) 56.
13. *Ibid.* 56.
14. *Ibid.* 62.

15. "The Divided Self; Jean Paul Sartre to R.D. Laing," in *Maps of the Mind*, ed. Charles Hampden Turner (New York: Mitchell Beazley, 1980) 46.
16. Hartley Lodwick, "Katherine Anne Porter," *Sewanee Review*, XLVIII (April, 1940) 214.
17. James Hemming, *Problems of Adolescent Girls* (London: Heinemann, 1960) 154.
18. M. Rosenburg, *Society and the Adolescent Self-image* (Princeton, N.J.: Princeton UP, 1965).
19. *Ibid.*
20. Katherine Anne Porter, "The Fig Tree." *Harper Magazine* (CXX, June 1960) 55-60.
21. *Ibid.* 114.
22. R.J. Evans, *Dialogue with Erik Harrison* (New York: Harper & Row, 1967).
23. L. Kohlberg & C. Gilligan, The adolescent as a philosopher: The discovery of the self in a post-conventional world, *Daedalus*, Fall 1971, 1066-67.
24. D. Elkind, *Children and Adolescents: Interpretative Essays on Jean Piaget* (New York: OUP, 1970).
25. P.H. Mussen, J.J. Conger & J. Kagan, *Child Development & Personality* (New York: Harper & Row) 1969 (3rd ed.) 696.
26. "The Days Before," *Kenyan Review*, V (Autumn, 1943) 492.
27. *Outline of Mexican Popular Arts and Crafts* (Los Angles: Young & M'Callister, Inc., 1922) 39.
28. "The Days Before," *Kenyan Review*, V (Autumn, 1943) 494.
29. C. Hugh Holman, "The Rebirth of the South: Wolfe Faulkner, Warren," *Modern American Literature.*
30. *Ibid.*
31. Frank Musgrove, *Youth and the Social Order* (Bloomington, Ind: Indiana UP, 1965) 126-27.
32. Karl Mannheim, *Essays on the Sociology of Culture* (New York: OUP, 1965).
33. John L. Stewart, *The Burden of Time: The Fugives and Agrarians* (Princeton: Princeton UP, 1965) 96.
34. William Faulkner, *Requiem for a Nun* (Middlesex: Penguin Books, 1970) 81.
35. B.D. Lorch, "The Perception of Deviancy by Self and Others," *Sociology and Social Research*, 50: 223-29.
36. W.W. Cruze, *Adolescent Psychology and Development* (The Ronald Press Company, New York, 1953).
37. Ira J. Gordon, *Human Development—A Transactional Perspective.* New York: Harper, 1962.

38. D. Ausubel & H. Schiff, Some Interpersonal and intrapersonal determinants of individual differences in socio-empathic ability among adolescents, *Journal of Social Psychology*, 1955, 41, 39-56.

39. D. Cooper, *Death of the Family* (New York: Pantheon, 1970).

40. J.B. Cooper, Parent evaluation as related to social ideology and academic achievement, *J. Genet. Psychol.*, 1962, 101, 135-43.

41. M. Mead, *Culture and Commitment: A study of the generation gap* (New York: Doubleday, 1970).

42. Robert Penn Warren, *Selected Essays* (New York: Random House, 1958) 153-54.

43. E.A. Dovvan & J. Adelson, *The Adolescent Experience* (New York: Wiley, 1966) 85.

44. P. Blos, 'The second individuation process of adolescence,' *Psychoanalytic Study of the Child*, 22, 178.

45. *Ibid.* 174.

46. James William Johnson, "Another Look at Katherine Anne Porter," *Virginia Quarterly Review*, 36 (Autumn, 1960) 602.

47. James O. Palmer, *The Psychological Assessment of Children*.

48. E.H. Erikson, *Identity: Youth and Crisis* (New York: Norton, 1968).

49. J. Joel Moss and Ruby Gingles, "The Relationship of Personality to the Incidence of Early Marriage," *Marriage and Family Living*, 21 (November, 1959) 377.

50. Samuel H. Lowrier, "Early Marriage: Premarital Pregnancy and Associated Factors," *Journal of Marriage and the Family*, 27 (February 1965) 53.

51. J. Joel Moss and Ruby Gingles, "A Preliminary Report of a Longitudinal Study of Early Marriages in Nebraska," Paper read at the Midwestern Sociological Society Convention in Minneapolis (April 27, 1958).

52. Wendell Johnson, *People in Quandaries* (New York: Harper & Bros., 1964) 14, 18, 488.

53. J. Piaget, *The Moral Judgement of the Child* (New York: Harcourt, Brace, 1932) 133-34.

54. Robert Penn Warren, "Irony with a Centre: Katherine Anne Porter," *Selected Essays* (New York: Random House, 1958) 283.

55. K. Keniston, *The Uncommitted: Alienated Youth in American Society* (New York: Dell, 1960) 396-98.

56. L.S. Feuer, *The Conflict of Generations* (New York: Basic Books, 1969).

57. Karl Mannheim, *Essays on the Sociology of Culture* (New York: OUP, 1956) 165.

58. R. Nixon, "Psychological Normality in the Years of Youth, *Teachers College Record*, 66: 71-74, 1964.

59. Winston Ehrmann, "Changing Sexual Mores," *Values and Ideals of American Youth* ed. Eli Ginzberg (New York: Columbia UP, 1964) 53-70.

60. William L. Nance, *Katherine Anne Porter and the Art of Rejection* (Chapel Hill: University of North Carolina P, 1964) 96.
61. Arthur W. Calhoun, *A Social History of the American Family: Colonial Period* (New York: Barnes and Noble, 1960) I, 132.
62. August Bebel, *Women in the Past, Present and Future.* Trans. H.B. Adams Walther (London: Modern P, 1885).
63. Dorothy S. Redden, "Flowering Judas: Two Voices," *Studies in Short Fiction,* 6 (Winter 1969) 195.
64. Katherine Anne Porter, *The Days Before* (New York: Harcourt Brace, 1952) 129.
65. Katherine Anne Porter, "Katherine Mansfield: Fictional Method," *Nation,* 1937, 86.
66. Maxwell Gismar, Tragic *Versus* Comic America: Society and the Novel, *Modern American Literature.*
67. Cleanth Brooks, "The Southern Temper" in *A Shaping Joy: Studies in the Writer's Craft* (New York: Harcourt Brace, 1971) 205-08.
68. Elizabeth Janeway, "Women's Literature," in *Harvard Guide to Contemporary American Writing* ed. Daniel Hoffman (Delhi: OUP, 1979) 344.
69. Robert Penn Warren, "Katherine Anne Porter: Irony with a Center," *Kenyon Review* 4 (1942) 29-42 rpt. in Katherin Anne Porter, ed. Hartley and Lane, 51-66.
70. Jane Addams, *The Spirit of Youth and the City Streets* (New York: Macmillan, 1910) 5-6.
71. Lydall Gorden, *Virginia Woolf: A Writer's Life* (Oxford: OUP, 1984) 256.
72. Gilbert Seldes, *New Republic* October 21, 1925.
73. cf. Sigmung Freud, *Beyond the Pleasure Principle,* 1922.
74. John Edward Hardy, *Katherine Anne Porter* 69.
75. Robert E. Grinder, "Socialization: Adolescence and Society," *Studies in Adolescence.*
76. J.V. Mitchell, Jr., "Goal-Setting Behaviour as a Function of Self-Acceptance over- and underachievement and Related Personality Variables," *Journal of Educational Psychology,* 50: 93-104, 1959.

4

ADOLESCENCE IN *THE CATCHER IN THE RYE*

Growing up, for some people is an uneventful, gradual process. Many face life quite realistically, but hopefully. There are some adolescents, however, to whom growing up is a source of anxiety. They dread relinquishing childhood dependency and assuming responsibility for their own actions. Sometimes they feel completely overwhelmed by their problems. In these cases, previous blighting experiences make them hostile or excessively submissive. Some move against people; some move away from people into their own world of fantasy. The young adolescents have implied increasing "ego strength except in those cases in which the child is struggling with conflicts of such intensity that his ego is powerless to deal with them."[1]

Erik H. Erikson wrote in "Childhood and Society," "The adolescent mind is essentially a mind of the moratorium, a psycho-social stage between childhood and adulthood, and between the morality learned by the child, and the ethics developed by the adult. It is an ideological mind—and indeed it is the ideological outlook of a society that speaks most clearly to the adolescent who is eager to be confirmed by his peers, and is ready to be confirmed by the rituals, creeds and programs which at the same time define what is evil, uncanny, and inimical."[2] But mostly in the name of ideology, the "rituals, creeds and programs" that help define the adult, a vacuum remaining which is filled by the adolescent's peers. The adolescent who is given nothing by society to assure him of first-class membership, has fewer defenses against the facts and panics than anyone else. As Jung wrote, "Resistance to the organized mass can be effected only by the man who is as well-organized in his individuality as the mass itself. I realize that this proposition must sound well-nigh unintelligible to the man of today."[3]

The Catcher in the Rye is neither a story of social rebellion nor one of philosophical quest. Holden, the central character whose experiences provide the subject-matter of the novel, is neither a revolutionary nor a saint or seeker of truth. He is an American adolescent facing a psychological crisis and in desperate search of personal relationships powerful enough to pull him through. The search which ends, after a series of frustrations, in Holden's surrender to his child-sister Phoebe, is the basis of the novel's unity as well as the source of its tensions.[4]

Keats, one of Salinger's favourite poets who knew more than any one else the agonies of adolescence, in his preface to *Endymion* has an interesting passage which could be of great help to us in our efforts to understand Holden:

> The imagination of a boy is healthy, and the mature imagination of a man is healthy; but there is a space of life between in which the soul is inferment, the character undecided, the way of life uncertain, the ambition thick-sighted; thence proceed mankishness and the thousand bitters.[5]

One of the most important sources of Holden's difficulties is his immaturity. Antolini, his history teacher, suggest this to him, when he quotes from Wilhelm Stekel; "The mark of the immature man is that he wants to die nobly for a cause, while the mark of mature man is that he wants to live humbly for one" (169). Many of Holden's attitudes to things and people are characterized by immaturity. Very often the immaturity is the direct result of the illusion of maturity from which Holden suffers. Holden rejects knowledge because he believes that it can only buy Cadillacs. He pursues wisdom but this search, instead of bringing him illumination, succeeds only in leading him to the verge of madness.

We may not like Carl Luce, but there is definitely a point when he asked Holden, "When in hell are you going to grow up?" (131). Holden's crisis is the result of isolation. Its immediate cause is his getting the axe at Prency Prep and his ostracising by the school fencing team. Holden at Prency Prep can be taken as the young American in his natural setting, a character and a milieu which are strongly individualized and yet in an important sense representative. He is shown as a complete misfit there. School is the place where the immature is socialized for entry into the approved adult activities; and so a boy's relation to his school becomes a microcosm of the individual's relation to his society.

Holden's hatred for schools and games shows his rejection of the ethos of his society. He dislikes his headmaster and Spencer for their insistence that life is a game, boy...' (7). He says:

> Game my ass. Some game. If you get one the side where all the hot-shots are, then it's a game, all right—I admit that. But if you get on the other side, where there aren't any hot-shots, then what's a game about? Nothing. No game. (71)

The games, as he sees, is the glorification of success and callousness towards failure.

During the farewell lecture, Holden is restless, bored—"I moved my ass a little but on the bed"—and then suddenly uneasy, "I felt sorry as hell for him all of a sudden. But I just couldn't hang around there any longer." This refrain echoes through the narrative; and the rebellious young hero ends up being "sorry" for all the jerks, morons, and queers who seem to populate the fashionable and preparatory school world.

The novel protests, to be sure, against both the academic and social conformity of its period. When Holden mopes about the New York museum which is almost the true home of his discredited childhood, he remembers the Indian war—canoes "about as long as three goddam cadillacs in a row." He refuses any longer to participate in the wealthy private boys' schools where "...all you do is talk about girls and liquor and sex all day, and everybody sticks together in these dirty little goddam cliques" (43). The novel presents all the petty horrors, the banalities, the final mediocrity of the typical American Prep school.

Arthur L. Stinchombe writes: "When a student realizes that he does not achieve status increment from improved current performance, current performance loses meaning. The student becomes hedonistic because he does not visualize achievement of long-run goals through current self-restraint. He reacts negatively to conformity that offers nothing concrete. He claims autonomy from adults because their authority does not promise him a satisfactory future."[5]

Holden flees Prency Prep before he is expelled, and comes to New York to have three days of freedom before he joins his family. "One of the biggest reason I left Elkton Hills was because I was surrounded by phonies. That's all. They were coming in the goddam window. I can't stand that stuff. It drives me crazy. It makes me so depressed I go crazy" (12). He wants to make a world of his own. "He dreams of running away and building his own cabin where people could do anything but phony when they visited me. If anybody tried to do anything phony, they could not stay" (179).

Many schools tend to emphasize what Silberman calls "education for docility." Too often it appears, they overemphasize order, discipline and conformity, at the expense of self-expression, intellectual curiosity, creativity and the development of a humane, sensitive human being who is concerned with values, capable of self-reliance and independent judgment, and able and willing to learn for himself.

There are a variety of reasons for discrepancies between the potential dropout's intelligence and his basic academic skills: deficiencies in home background, in motivation, in emotional adjustment, in the appropriateness of his teaching and the like. Once academic difficulties have developed, however, they exert a formidable influence of their own.

In several studies, dropouts have emerged as more troubled emotionally, less confident of their own worth, lower in self-esteem, more lacking in a clearly defined self-image and sense of identity, and less likely to have structure values and goals—personal, social or occupation—than graduates. They are more likely to have hostile, angry feelings and to be resentful of authority in any form—"home authority, civil authority, intellectual authority, occupational authority."[7]

Influenced more by frustrations from which they are trying to escape than by longer-term goals toward which they are striving, these adolescents tend to live more for the moment, responding impulsively, planning little, showing little sustained, goal-directed activity, and seeking immediate gratification.[8]

According to projective tests, dropouts are more likely to view the world as an unpredictable place, characterized by violence, hostility, strife, cheating, faithlessness and exploitation of other people. In this world as perceived by the dropouts, longer term goals are rather meaningless. Plans are likely to go astray or to be doomed from the start. In this approach to life, L.F. Cervantes observes:

> Human relations are characteristically brittle, haphazard, unpremediated, affectless, and exploitative.... Gratitude is a superfluous theme. Fun, pleasure, spontaneity and emotional upheavals of various types are much in evidence but not as integrated with the superphysical or with life's goals. Our dropout protocols seem more interlaced with the impulse ridden, the non-deferred gratification, the unconventional, the unrealistically romantic, the loosely structured, the shallow, the predestined, the fateful.
> ...the mind of the dropout seems to exhale feelings of inadequacy, worthlessness, frustration, and failure.[9]

Thus dropping out of school is more likely to be the result of an adolescent's problems than their cause. The greatest challenge is not to keep a young person in a school situation that is unrewarding, irrelevant or destructive, but to ameliorate the conditions that led to dropping out in the first place. And for those who have already dropped out, we need to develop more appropriate opportunities and guidance.

Holden, too, fails to get the guidance he needs from his teachers or from the parents. Nor is there any religious guidance in the form of school chaplin or family minister. On the failure of religion, Holden tells us, "my parents are of different religions, and all the children in our family are atheists. If you want to know the truth, I can't even stand ministers.... They sound so phony when they talk." And, about his family, Holden explains, "my parents would have about two haemorrhages apiece if I told anything pretty personal about them" (1). So Holden cannot get advice on how to leave the world of childhood.

Finch agrees that the roots of adolescent disturbances extend far back into childhood, but he stresses the adolescent era as the period in which an actual psychotic reaction is first likely to develop. He suggests, that coping behaviours which allow a preschizophrenic youngster to maintain a limited but reasonable adjustment during his relatively dependent childhood years may first prove to be inadequate at adolescence, when the increased psychological pressures of the teenage years begin to disrupt his personality integration.[10]

The adolescent who describes bizarre fantasies or strange dreams may be experiencing a schizophrenic disturbance; yet this likelihood rests primarily with the extent to which such material is recounted in a blocked, dissociated, or circumstantial manner that demonstrates formal thought disorder. Wilson (1951) has elaborated the diagnostic significance of a disturbed adolescent's reaction to the content of his thoughts in relation to obsessive—compulsive phenomena which frequently overlap neurotic disturbances. He observes that "in the non-psychotic person, obsessional anxiety is accompanied by some awareness of the symptom's abnormality,"[11] as reflected in such comments as, "I know it's ridiculous to have this idea, but I just can't get it out of my head" (11).

Finding that almost the whole of the adult world is 'phony,' Holden rejects the very ideal of achieving adulthood, for the time being at least. He is confused and perplexed by the complexity, deviousness and lack of genuine love in adult society. Therefore, in disgust he seeks escape in a kind of protracted childhood. The people Holden admires most are kids or adults influenced by kids. Highest on the list of people he admires is Allie, his kid brother who died of leukaemia. Next comes James Castle, the boy he knew at Elkton Hills, who preferred death to taking back something he had said. His kid sister Phoebe prevents Holden from running away from home and society, and even in effecting a cure of his neurosis. Then again, it is a little six-year-old boy walking behind his uncaring parents in a crowded New York Street, and singing Robert Burns' song 'Coming thru the Rye' that gives Holden the idea of becoming a catcher in the rye. In his own private vision, this little catcher in the rye sees only those "thousands of little children" all playing near the dangerous cliff," and nobody's around—nobody big, I mean—except me" to rescue them from their morbid fate.

Holden's fantasies and visions of his future are closer to the truth and result in a deflating rather than an inflating of the ego. Time and again he calls himself a 'crazy bastard.' He realizes that he is a chronic liar. He admits the possibility of his being cowardly. In his case there is no attempt to gloss over unpalatable facts about himself or others. This ability to face facts is very useful to Holden. It may be one of the contributing factors in the achievement of his initiation in spite of his nervous breakdown. He realizes that he is terribly immature when confronted with a practical situation. He perceives very clearly the limitations and the phoniness of the people around him. At the same time he recognizes his own limitations and shortcomings. He admits there are many things he does not understand—the ducks in the pond in Central Park, adult society, the world and himself. This is a valuable insight about himself. For instance, though he knows quite a bit about sex (he distinguishes between perversion and normal sex behaviour among the inmates of his hostel), he is not sexually initiated. He is still a virgin, not only because he can't bring himself to take advantage of the girls but also because he does not understand sex. "Sex is something I really don't understand too hot. You never know where the hell you are. I keep making up these sex rules for myself, and then I break them right away" (56). He recognizes the strong sex urges in himself. 'I was feeling pretty horny. I have to admit it' (56). At the same time he recognizes the need to protect the young from sexual vice—the need to be a moral catcher in the rye, and rub out obscenities from school and museum walls. Throughout the novel there is a consistent preoccupation with innocence, a preference for pure love. It is in children and nuns only that Holden finds purity of love, divorced from sex. William Wiegand has observed that in Salinger's words, "Where object of delight is found in women, these women are often little girls or nuns and what is admired is sexless in essence."[12]

The adolescent's life is certainly not free from moral conflict and may be unusually troubled at times by the need for moral decisions regarding which he feels inadequate. At the same time, he makes choices where moral issues are involved without realizing what the alternatives and their values are. As Havighurst and Taba say: "The ability to apply moral beliefs to an increasing range of conflicting life situations is quite undeveloped at the age of sixteen.... They find conflicts hard to face; they tend to solve conflicts by using slogans rather than by using concepts of the relative significance of values."[13]

Chave defines morality in this way: "Morality is the self-regulation of conduct with due consideration for both one's own welfare and the welfare of others." He further says: "One cannot be moral until one recognizes the social consequences of one's acts, and one is moral to the degree that one controls one's conduct with concerns for these consequences." Putting it another way, he says: "Speaking generally, one may say that an act is right to the degree that it furthers the rights and welfare of all those involved in the act and that it is wrong to the degree that it hinders the welfare and growth of anyone."[14]

But everyone should be able to make moral choices upon the basis of his own judgment, for a social code can never be so flexible or so minutely detailed as to take care of every situation. As Chave says: "While most of a person's conduct may be guided by conventional mores, progress depends upon revision of conventional practices and requires keen judgment."[15] Feuer cites Plato's view that generational struggle constitutes the primary mechanism in social change, and Aristotle's assertion that political revolutions are caused "not only by the conflict of rich and poor, but by the struggle between sons and fathers."[16]

Murray, in an article, "Time for a Positive Morality," stresses the fact that our social philosophy has had a negative orientation and it is time for us to stress a positive ideal of moral development. We have been able to agree on what we *don't* want, he says, but have not been able to agree on what we *do* want. He suggests that instead of setting up a lofty image of perfection as a spur to our efforts, we should work out clearly the steps to attaining it; instead of preaching moral absolutes, we should define the conditions under which they should operate; instead of imposing ideals from above, we should devise a democratic way of modifying and improving outselves.[17] Holden has his own uncompromising ideals—ideals about other people and about what the world should be. It is these ideals which are so disturbing for the adult reader and which are such easy targets for the common dismissal of Holden as "an immature kid who needs to grow up and face reality." It is these very ideals and Holden's rage against the impossibility of attaining the ideals which have so endeared Holden to adolescent readers or those young adults who still fondly recall their 'initiation into evil.' Holden feels that what really is important, is something like refusing to take back a statement that you know is true. He knows that integrity and honesty are important. He knows that barring pimpy guys from secret clubs is wrong—just because they are human beings too... (151). Telling to Phoebe, why had he flanked out of Penecy, he says:

> Oh God, Phoebe, don't ask me. I'm sick of everybody asking me that. A million reasons why. It was one of the worst schools I ever went to. It was full of phonies. And mean guys. You never saw so many mean guys in your life. For instance, if you were having a bull session in somebody's room, and somebody wanted to come in, no body'd let them in if they were some dopey, pimpy guy. Everybody was locking their door when somebody wanted to come in. And they had this goddam secret fraternity that I was too yellow not to join. There was this one pimply, boring guy, Rober Ackley, that wanted to get in. He kept trying to join, and they wouldn't let him. I don't even feel like talking about it. It was a stinking school. Take my word (151).

Holden Caulfield is Salinger's typical quixotic hero in search of the simple truth. He is rather in flight from mendacity than in search of truth, and his sensitivity to the failures of the world is compounded with his self-disgust. The fact that he longs to be a catcher in the rye indicates his capacity for love and compassion. He showers his love on children and occasionally on adults, too. At times, his compassion becomes comparable to the great compassion of the Budha, Holden constantly worries about the ducks in Central Park. The adults he meets during his wanderings in New York are not able to give a satisfactory answer to his queries. On the contrary, they make him for a nut for having asked them. It is a concern that adults just cannot share, and when this truth dawns on him, he comes to the conclusion that adults cannot love. He agrees with the statement that Salinger uses, 'Hell is the suffering of being unable to love.'

There are many other indications of Holden's compassion. He feels sorry for almost everyone he meets, even the ones who cause him pain and grief. He feels sorry for his old history teacher, Spencer, who flunks him because he has cut a sorry figure in the examination. He has a great compassion for the two nuns he meets on the train because they cannot afford a respectable breakfast while he himself eats a lavish one. Impulsively he makes a contribution of ten dollars to them. He feels sorry for all the girls he meets, Sally Hayes and Jane Gallagher and even the young prostitute, Sunny. It is his compassion for girls that is the reason for his virginity even at the age of seventeen. He just cannot bring himself to take advantage of the girls. He is kind to repulsive Ackley, with his "sinus trouble, pimples, lousy teeth, halitosis and crumby fingernails." He also obviates Slagle's envy of his Mark Cross luggage. Most significantly, for an adolescent undergoing the torturing growing pains of sex, he sympathizes with the girl's situation—with the ugly daughter of Pencey's headmaster, with both the ugly girl and the beautiful girl in the night club, with the prostitute Sunny, with the girl Luce has enjoyed and now derogates and with Jane Gallagher whose fear Holden appreciates. It is his compassion again that accounts for the very strange advice he gives at the end of the book: "About all I know is, I sort of *miss* everybody I told about. Even old Stradlater and Ackley, for instance.... Don't ever tell anybody anything. If you do, you start missing everybody" (192).

Kenneth Keniston argues in *The Uncommitted: Alienated Youth in American Society* that modern society, far from fostering homogeneity and a premature closure of identity—seeking in adolescents, is rather serving increasingly to alienate youth from adult value-systems. He maintains that a technological society, because of its chronic social change and fragmentation, holds neither clarity nor attraction for its young people:

> They know the adult world they expect to enter with a subtle distrust, a lack of high expectations, hopes or dreams, and an often unstated feeling that they will have to "settle" for less than they would hope for it they let themselves hope.... Essentially, they recognize that adulthood is a relatively cold, demanding, specialized, and abstracted world where "Meaningful" work is so scarce they do not even ask for it.... The adult world, then as seen from within the youth culture inspires neither enthusiasm nor commitment.[18]

Thus Keniston sees the youth as struggling though their adolescence without commitment, with a disaffection from adulthood, and with a limited sense of what they are. Keniston predicts that youth will increasingly have "a special culture of its with characteristics that are those of neither childhood nor adulthood."[19]

Robins believes that there are fairly firm criteria for predicting which children will develop a behaviour problem. He says: "We know that psychiatric illness in the parents is reflected in an elevated rate of behaviour: problems in their children, and that anti-social parents have anti-social children. When the parents' anti-social behaviour takes the form of physical abuse of the child, the child shows very severe disability."[20] Nash K. Burger, too has the same assessment for Holden's behaviour. He finds him "Bwildered, lonely, ludicrous and pitiful," and at the same time finds that "his troubles, his failings are not of his own making but of a world that is out of joint. There is nothing wrong with him that a little understanding and affection, preferably from his parents, couldn't have set right.... His delinquencies seem minor indeed when contrasted with the adult delinquencies with which he is confronted."[21]

Arthur Heiserman and James E. Miller, Jr., feel that the theme of the novel is the questing child, who cannot escape society. His quest is especially difficult because his innocence, does not enable him to adjust to what Frederic J. Carpenter terms, "the ambivalence of American society." Such ambivalence affects the nature of the quest itself, which becomes both a "flight from" and a "quest for."[22]

The stresses of post-industrial society are also one of the causes of psychic disturbances in adolescents. In a book by the cultural critic Christopher Lasch, *Haven in a Heartless World: The Family Besieged*, we see the various anxieties that have developed within the nuclear family:

> Films, comic strips, and popular novels—in particular the many novels of adolescents revolt, patterned after J.D. Salinger's "The Catcher in the Rye"—ridicule the 'manifest' father, and authority in general while depicting 'latent' father—figures as sinister, aggressive and utterly unprincipled in their prosecution of their hero or heroine.

The world of *The Catcher in the Rye* is a post-industrial world of leisure and the decline of parental authority. Holden's father is a busy and very rich lawyer. Holden seems to exist in a world almost entirely composed of leisure pursuits. His usual milieu is one in which he is socializing with his peer group. He himself says: "Sometimes I horse around quite a lot, just to keep from getting bored" (21). Through Holden Salinger wants to show that the adolescent culture is breaking up under the pressure of a society in which there is too much of leisure. He shows a world in which the loafing habits of adolescents have become a way of life. Endicott Peadbody, warning against the dangers of the kind of peer group interaction that is a daily ritual for Holden, writes:

> It seems to me of the utmost importance that there should be nothing of the nature of loafing in a school. The curse of American College life and of school life is

> loafing. Boys and men get together in a sociable way and sit around a room and talk and gossip, and a little scandal comes in, and then evil. The tone of loafers is always low.[23]

Salinger indirectly presents the tragic state of Holden's world. The following passage reflects the marooned status of Holden and his fellows within modern America:

> Youth are segregated from adults by the economic and educational institutions created by adults; they are deprived of psychic support from persons of the ages, a psychic support that once came from the family; they are subordinate and powerless in relation to adults, and outsiders to the dominant social institutions.[24]

In the preface of his book *The Lonely Crowd: A Study of the Changing American Character,* Riesman suggest that social influence should and can be positive and supportive and is probably essential: "In order that any society may function well, its members must acquire the kind of character which makes them want to act in the way that they have to act as members of the society or of a special class within it."[25] Reisman believed that external agencies of socialization, like the school, could have a creative influence on the development of children. The healthy growth of a human personality is possible in the social group only.

The home wields a powerful influence over the attitudes and behaviour of young people. In fact, behaviour patterns of childhood, whether they are good or bad, tend to become intensified as the individual develops and matures, unless environmental factors stimulate changes.

Adolescence, infact, is a training period for both the parent and the child. If the parent is able to adjust his own attitudes and behaviour to the needs of his growing boy or girl, the latter will be helped immensely in the solution of those problems which are inherent to the growing-up process.

Holden sees in his society the possibilities for horror and depravity on a massive scale. It has very few chances of profound satisfaction. He sees life as self-destructive. He feels himself to be homeless, frozen out like the ducks in the Central

Park. The memories of Allie and the companionship of Phoebe are the only sources of affection. He is one of the loneliest characters, desperately in need of love. He does not want to grow up in a society where human relationships are measured in terms of social status and money income. He is seeking a deeper, more real relationship with someone—a more human relationship. When Sally explains to Holden about his obligation to fulfil the traditional male role of husband and dreams of "...Oodles of marvellous places to go" (119). Holden gives us the idea of his future which haunts him and which is one more factor preventing him from "growing up" into the society:

> I said, no there wouldn't be marvellous places to go to after I went to college and all. Open your ears. It'd be entirely different. We'd have to go downstairs in elevators with suitcases and stuff. We'd have to phone up everybody and tell 'em goodbye and send 'em postcards from hostels and all. And I'd be working in some office, making a lot of dough, and riding to work in cabs and Madison Avenue Buses, and reading newspapers, and playing bridge all the time, and going to the movies (119).

Some critics have described Holden's thoughts as childish self-inflations. They regard him as a mere neurotic whose psychopathic self-righteousness and puritanism have mercifully left him with a competent psychiatrist.[26] But adolescence is not necessarily, as was believed at one time, a period of constant stress and strain. Usually young people are helped to experience a gradual continuum of development from early childhood to adulthood. There are conditions and situations in the lives of most teenagers, however, when the apparent thwarting of strong urges, impulses or ambitions may stimulate the arousal of severe emotional disturbance. With self-awareness comes the struggle for self-realization. Social codes, unfulfilled desires, goals beyond achievement may cause mental and emotional disturbance.

In his book, *Adolescent Development and Adjustment*, Crow writes that "the adolescent becomes confused by the discrepancies in the moral codes to which he is exposed. Difficulties arise, however, when the apparent moral codes of the various groups with which he is associated differ so widely that his childhood-habituated behaviour is approved by the members of one group, tolerated by others, and condemned by still others."[27] Adolescents become increasingly aware of inconsistencies between what parents say and what they do, between the social world that has been described to them and the social world which they now begin to see for themselves. They need help in handling conflicting values and standards. Havighurst has reported evidence that character is related to parental consistency. Either extreme permissiveness or extreme severity seems to be less determinant to character formation than inconsistency of discipline.[28]

Holden affirms goodness, honesty and loyalty, though he does so with an agonizing self-consciousness and a bitter spirit. His perception of innocence is radical. With honest insight that looks down upon the sadistic practices and class discriminations, he remarks: "I can even get to hate somebody, just looking at them, if they have cheap suitcases with them...it is really hard to be roommates with people if your suitcases are much better than theirs...you think if they're intelligent...they don't give a damn whose suitcase are better, but they do. They really do" (98). He finds the modern world distorted. Almost everyone in his world is 'phony'—headmasters, students, movie actors, movie goers.

Holden is equally critical of snobbery wherever he finds it, whether it is in the headmaster or piano player, Ermie, or the Lunts or other actors. Old Hass, for example, is shown going around shaking hands with the parents of his students:

> He'd be charming as hell and all. Except if somebody had little funny looking parents.... I mean if a boy's mother was sort of fat or corny looking or something, and if somebody's father was one of those guys that wear those suits with very big shoulders and corny black and white shoes, then old Hass would just shake hand with them and give them a phoney smile and then he'd go talk, for may be a half an hour, with somebody else's parents. (12)

He is also critical of the piano-player Ermie's snobbery. He says: "He's a terrific snob and he won't hardly even talk to you unless you're a big shot or a celebrity or something" (72). He finds snobbery in the intellectuals also who "do not like to have an intellectual conversation with you unless they're running the whole thing" (132).

Harvey Breit calls Holden "a critique of the contemporary grown-up world."[29] In S.N. Behrman's observation, he "is driven crazy by 'phoniness,' a heading under which he loosely gathers not only insincerity but snobbery, injustice, callousness to the tears in things and a lot more."[30] He is intelligent enough to make out the difference between advertised qualities and the actual performance of his school:

> They advertise in about a thousand magazines, always showing some hot-shot guy on a horse jumping over a fence. Like as if all you ever did at Pency was play polo all the time. I never even once saw a horse anywhere *near* the place. And underneath the guy on the horse's picture, it always say: 'Since 1888 we have been molding boys into splendid, clear-thinking young men.' Strictly for the birds. They don't do any damn more *molding* at Pency than they do at any other school. And I didn't know anybody there that was splendid are clear thinking at all. May be two guys. If that many. And they probably *came* to Pency that way. (2)

Holden's visit to Spencer is the first of several efforts he makes to fight the crisis. Holden likes Old Spencer—the history teacher at Prencey—but the visit ends in failure and frustration because of Holden's revulsion at Spencer's "terrible posture," his "yelling," and his habit of picking his nose. Holden's next effort is with Stradlater, his roommate, with whom he has an ambivalent relationship. He is critical of Stradlater and dislikes him for his conceitedness and his technique with girls but he is also attracted to him because he is a 'very friendly guy' and has a sense of humour. Holden's conversation with Stradlater in the Can, where he follows him, and his fight with him later over Jane Gallagher show Holden's attempts to establish some kind of relationship with him. This attempt, which ends more miserably than before, brings out Holden's immaturity in matters of sex. A powerful factor involved in his fight with Stradlater is the sexual jealousy which arises out of the highly ambiguous statements that Stradlater gives about the details of his dating with Jane. This fight also brings in another of Holden's concerns, the agonies of adolescence. From here he escapes to New York to search there for sexual adventure. Brain Way writes:

> ...describes Holden's four successive attempts at sexual satisfaction: his telephone-call to the girl who is 'not quite a whore': his evening in the Lavender Room with the three girls from Seattle, Washington; his encounter with the prostitute; and his proposal to Sally Hayes.... Holden's excitement is the excitement of the fantasist: he is embarking on a dream which is both universally adolescent, and build into contemporary American mass-culture through Hollywood and television, advertising, pulp fiction and magazines, and social mores—the offer of unbelievable possibilities of sexual adventure and satisfaction. This erotic day-dream is confronted in each of the four incidents with harsh realities which the day-dream disqualifies.... Holden is caught in an ironic and painful dialectic: four time his participation in the communal day-dream propel him into real situations from which he recoils, even more incapacitated and humiliated, back into fantasy.[31]

Holden's attitude to sex has the same ambivalence as his attitude to movies, to night clubs and to many other things. He hates sex, but allows his mind to be obsessed by it. Unlike the grown up Stradlater or Carl Luce, he is not mature enough to establish normal and satisfactory sex-relationships, though he likes girls and women. But in his desperate search of companionship, he gets involved in several sex adventures. He often lies about his age. This shows that there is an urge in Holden, though at the unconscious level, to play the adult in order to imitate Stradlater.

Salinger is from the start an extremely moral writer, and sexual morality is no small part of his moral vision. Salinger is concerned with how people treat one another and whether it is possible for them to deal with one another in kindness.

For many of his characters, love is simply impossible, that is what makes sex so negative a factor in his work.

Brain Way writes "The strength of Salinger's study of adolescence is that he does not stop with a succession of superficial manifestations as other novelists have done, but goes straight to the fundamental biological situation. He sees that all the contradictions, agonies, and exaltations of adolescence stem from the central fact: that the adolescent has newly gained the physical potentialities for sexual experience but has not learnt to integrate them either within himself or in any consistent relation to the demands of society."[32]

The Sunny episode brings out some important aspects of Holden's personality—his desperate need to find some kind of relationship and his inability to find it in sex. Holden's courageous but strange stand against Maurice results in torture, physical as well as psychological, and leaves him in a sad plight. There is a horrified awareness of physical process in the hands of a calculating prostitute.

Holden's meeting with the nuns at the Sandwich Bar and his attempts to communicate with them, especially the nuns with glasses, are very important in the structure of the novel. Holden's gift of money to the nuns represents his ability to discover the "nice things" in the Inverted Forest, Salinger's symbol for the contemporary human situation. Holden has a prejudice against all institutions and groups, including the religious, but they do not interfere in his relations with human beings.

The Sally Hayes episode marks the beginning of an acute stage in Holden's neurosis. Sally's enthusiasm for her boy friend Andover, "George something" upsets Holden. It arouses the feeling of sexual jealousy in him. The humiliation which has a terrible effect on Holden's nerves results in his violet outburst against people in general. Holden seeks refuge from this fury in his private world of fantasy and makes a fantastic proposal to Sally that they should run away. Sally's refusal, which destroys this fantasy, results in his final insult to her. The Sally Hayes episode is yet another illustration of Holden's ambivalent attitude to sex and his immaturity in dealing with its problems. It also provides an explosive self-revelation, in which Holden admits that he is crazy and swears to God that he is a madman. Earlier in a fight with Stradlater Holden was "practically yelling"; and here he expresses his urge to withdraw from society.

In fact, Holden is snobbish in ways peculiar to adolescence. He never knows exactly what any girl may be expecting of him and is afraid to make love to the prostitute supplied by an obliging bellhop. He mistakes whatever is spontaneous in his behaviour for madness: "But I'm crazy. I swear to God I'm." If he acts on impulse he feels guilty, though also boastful: "I'm the most terrific liar you ever saw in your life" (14).

Kohlberg points out, "the child's sexual identity is maintained by a motivated adaptation to physical social reality and by the need to preserve a stable and positive self-image." He further writes that "many conceptualizations and research findings on self-consistency and on dissonance reduction or cognitive balance support the view that people tend to seek cognitive consistency."[33]

'Storm and Stress' are instantly recognizable phrases applying to the adolescent period of human development. G. Stanley Hall, an early writer on adolescence, is often credited with being the first to propose this theory. Weiner quotes Hall as writing thus in 1904:

> The teens are emotionally unstable and pathic. It is the age of natural inebriation without the needs of intoxicants, which made Plato define youth as a spiritual drunkenness. It is a natural impulse to experience hot and perforative psychic states, and it is characterized by emotionalism. We see here the instability and fluctuations now so characteristic. The emotions develop by contrast and reaction into the opposite.[34]

Almost all later psychoanalytic writing has supported this view. Ackerman is another writer who proposes a thesis which exemplifies the 'storm and stress' point of view; he argues that much of adolescence is characterized by anti-social behaviour, sexual promiscuity, over-conformity with peers, disillusionment, despair and disorientation in relation with family and community. Ackerman's belief is that much of this behaviour is due to the instability of the modern family, which does not provide, according to him, the security necessary for optimal emotional growth.[35] Thus it becomes apparent that adolescence is a time of life at which very considerable disruption is to be expected. Further, this perspective relates to the large majority of adolescents rather than being true only of the relative minority who make up the clinical population.

Holden Caulfield faces a society in which there seems to be no place for him, particularly since it is a society structure to accommodate adults. Deep-rooted in materialism, modern American society is repelling towards a value-seeker like Holden. He is sickened by the material values and inhumanity of the world around him. And in the whole novel we find him struggling to get an order of morality and a possibility of love within this world. He is repulsed by materialism because people prefer material goods to human beings.

> Take most people. They're crazy about cars. They worry if they get a little scratch on them, and they are always talking about how many miles they get to a gallon, and if they get a brand new car already they start thinking about trading it in for one that is even newer. I don't even like old cars. I mean they don't even interest me. I'd rather have a goddam horse. A horse is at least human, for God's sake...." (117)

The slangy, idiomatic, frequently vulgar language which Salinger puts in the mouth of his hero is worth quoting. Holden's twentieth-century prep-school vernacular, despite its obscenities, manages to communicate ideas and feelings of a quite complex sort. His incorrect spellings suggest a subconscious will to non-conformity. He has an "educated" vocabulary and speaks with a modern school-boy's idiom and slang. Most critics thought that this language is a true and authentic rendering of teenage colloquial speech, the speech of an educated North-eastern American adolescent. Donald P. Costello feels that his typical speech is overlaid with strong personal idiosyncrasies. The two major speech habits, which are Holden's own, are endlessly repeated throughout the book and are typical enough of teenage speech. He further adds that it is common for teenagers to end thoughts with a loosely dangling 'and all,' just as it is common for them to add an insistent. 'I really did,' 'It really was.'[36] For example:

...he's my brother and all (1)
...was in the Revolutionary War and all (2)
It was December and all (3)
...right in the pocket and all (3)
...they're nice and all (1)
...splendid and clear-thinking and all (2).

Donald Barr writes, "Salinger has an ear not only for idiosyncrasies of diction and syntax, but for mental processes. Holden Caulfield's phrase is 'and all'—'She looked so da nice, the way she kept going around and around in her blue coat and all'—as if each experience were a halo. His fallacy is *ab. uno disce omnes*; he abstracts and genealizes wildly.[37]

Heiserman and Miller comment on Holden's another idiosyncrasy: "In a phony world Holden feels compelled to reinforce his sincerity and truthfulness constantly with, 'It really is' or 'It really did.'"[38] Phrases like, 'If you really want to know,' or 'if you want to know the truth' although used casually become psychologically portentous. The inference is that society has no desire to recognize the truth about Holden or its own obsessions. S.N. Behrman thinks that these insistencies of Holden's reveal his age, even when he is thinking much older, and, more important, 'he is so aware of the danger of slipping into phoniness himself that he has to repeat over and over "I really mean it." "It really does."[39] These idiosyncrasies of Holden are in keeping with general teenage language.

His is a typical teenage slang: versatile, expressive, imprecise and crude. A typical aspect of Holden's language, according to Donald P. Costello, is that it shows the general American characteristic of adaptability—apparently strengthened by his teenage lack of restraint. He can very easily turn nouns into adjectives by adding a—y: 'perverty,' 'Christmasy,' 'Vomity-looking,' 'whory-looking,' 'hoolumy-looking,' 'show-offy,' 'dumpy-looking,' 'pimpy,' 'snobby,' 'fisty.' His habit of violating the grammar-rules and the use of repetitive vocabulary is the typical, informal, colloquial, teenage American speech.

From the psychological point of view, his mixing both the slob and the literate idiom becomes a self-protective acceptance of the slob values of his prep school contemporaries. Carl F. Strauch observes that the psychological intent becomes a symbolical portent when we see that the mass idiom emphasizes a significant distinction between two worlds—the phony world of corrupt materialism and Holden's private world of innocence, which in its corporate love, embraces a secret goldfish, his dead brother Allie, his sister Phoebe, Gallagher, nuns and animals. For his private world Holden uses a literate and expressive English; so the profound or psychological and symbolic purposes of slob language may be detected only as that idiom functions in polarized relationship with the other.[40] Holden's nervous, jerky reiteration often points up his emotional tensions. His sometimes jarring speech and tense outpouring expresses his psychological unrest. Hence, it is possible to say that his speech is indeed suited to his neurotic experience of the all-engulfing modern city. Edward P.J. Corbett discussing *The Catcher in the Rye* rightly argues that, "given the kind of character that figures as the hero, no other language was possible. The integrity of the novel demanded such language."[41]

Looking at society as perceived through the eyes of an adolescent, Salinger has painted a devastating picture. Holden does not find happiness in a simple, natural world, a world which is corrupted and insecure. He feels frustrated, and rootless in this twentieth century modern America. His nihilism is intensified as the modern metropolis as nightmare. He describes a night in New York city:

> ...it was so quiet and lonesome out, even though it was Saturday night. I didn't see hardly anybody on the street.... New York's terrible when somebody laughs on the street very late at night. (74)

Salinger's protagonists protest against an exclusively American society of affluence. The pervading theme in his writings is man *versus* society, the individual *versus* society or individual *versus* conformity. David L. Stevenson, for example, has seen in him a "mirror of crisis" of the mid-twentieth century American life. He says, Salinger "throws you back into your own problems or into an awareness of them in your contemporaries."[42] To Arthur Mizener, Salinger's conception of relations "is an impressive evidence of the way he fits into a major tradition of American literature, what might be called the effort to define the Good American, "by putting him against the American milieu."[43] Carol and Richard Ohmann believe that " *The Catcher in the Rye* is among other things a serious critical mimesis of bourgeois life in the Eastern United States, ca. 1950—of snobbery, privilege, class injury, culture as badge of superiority; sexual exploitation, education subordinated to status, warped social feeling, competitiveness, stunted human possibility...."[44]

Condition of human beings is also described very pitiably:

> The bellboy that showed me to the room was this very old guy around 65. He was even more depressing than the room was. He was one of those bald guys that comb all their hair over from the side to cover up their baldness. I'd rather be bald than do that. Anyway, what a gorgeous job for a guy around 65 years old. Carrying people's suitcases and waiting around for a tip. I suppose he won't be too intelligent or anything, but it was terrible anyway. (55)

Holden's loneliness is depressing. The element of isolation in the novel is emphasized in by him. Repulsed by the phoniness all-around him, he intends to become a deaf-mute:

> I figured I could get a job at filling station somewhere, putting gas and oil in people's cars. I didn't care what kind of job it was, though. Just so people didn't know me and i didn't know anybody. I thought what I'd do was, I'd pretend I was one of those deaf-mutes. That way I wouldn't have to have any goddam stupid useless conversation with anybody. If anybody wanted to tell me something, they'd have to write it on a piece of paper and show it over to me.... Everybody'd think I was just a poor deaf-mute bastard and they'd leave me alone.... I'd meet this beautiful girl that was also a deaf-mute and we'd get married. She'd come and live in my cabin with me and if she wanted to say anything to me she'd have to write it on a goddam piece of paper, like everybody else. (178-79)

Holden's hyper-sensitivity isolates him from his own age group and also from the adult world. As an adolescent, he finds it difficult to communicate with the phony adults. As a sensitive adolescent, he just cannot get along with his equals. He groves disillusioned and isolated, like the 'sad screwed up type guy' that he understands Shakespeare's *Hamlet* to be.

Ihab H. Hassan might have called the novel a "...revolt of the lonesome rich child, the conspicuous display of the leisure-class emotions."[45] But there is another category of critics like James Brayan,[46] Charles H. Kegel,[47] Peter J. Seng[48] and William Wiegand[49] who approach Salinger from the psychological, psychoanalytical stand. They try to find the drives which prompt Holden and other characters working under their kind of psychic pressures. They find that Salinger is writing about the mixed-up kids who are incestuous, hyper-sensitive and hyper-imaginative.

Psychologists have observed that many people become alienated from what they view as the hollowness and hypocrisy of many conventional social-relationships. Those who react by withdrawing into apathy and indifference are in a very different position from those who have attempted to find new and meaningful substitutes. Keniston writes that, "alienation can be expressed in many ways. In one sense the revolutionary and the psychotic are both highly alienated from the norms and values of their society—both reject these norms and values. Yet there is a vast difference in the way their rejection is expressed: the revolutionary actively attempts to transform his society; the psychotic has undergone a regressive self-transformation that leaves his society unaffected."[50]

In view of Keniston, the most prominently emphasized alienation currently involves an "explicit rejection of traditional American culture."[51] Some youth may respond to their alienation by withdrawing from the society as a whole. For some, this may involve deep despair or defeat, without any meaningful substitute to take the place of their alienations.

Coleman's views are in consistence with Keniston's description of alienated youth. In *The Adolescent Society* Coleman infers from a study of several thousand High school students that "the modern adolescent is experiencing a marginal existence between childhood and adulthood that requires him to look increasingly to his peers for his reward and values. Far from becoming prematurely assimilated into adult society," Coleman continues, "today's adolescents have developed their own teenage subculture replete with its own terminology, language and standards, all of which contribute to distinctly adolescent personality patterns: "He is 'cut off' from the rest of society, forced inward toward his own age group, made to carry out his whole social life with his own age. With his fellows, he comes to constitute a small society, one that has most of its important interactions within itself, and maintains only a few threads of connection with the outside adult society."[52]

Holden Caulfield has been called one of the loneliest characters in fiction. His feelings and thoughts isolate him from his friends, schoolmates, teachers and even strangers whom he meets. He is aware of his loneliness: "I felt so lonesome, all of a sudden. I almost wished I want dead" (46); "I got feeling so lonesome and rotten..." (42); "It made me too sad and lonesome" (43); "...it was so quite and lonesome out.... I kept wishing I could go home..." (43); "...I was feeling sort of lousy. Depressed and all. I almost wished I was dead" (42).

Depression is associated with adolescence, partly because periods of transition "...are as often as not experienced by the individual as private and lonely moments, not as high points, mutually shared by others in his community."[53] In addition, Konopka observes that adolescents are unusually vulnerable. Their attempts to explore their environment and to reach out for new experience explore intense emotions. If the outcomes of experimentation are negative, they suffer because they lack "a bank of positive experiences to draw from when defeats occur."[54]

All adolescents experience crisis in relation to their attitudes toward independence and sexuality; their feelings toward parents, peers, siblings, and themselves; and their definitions of their interests and motivations.

Another significant addition to the dynamic formulation of depression is contributed by Bibriny who postulates failure to realize one's aspirations as the essential element in depressive disorders:

> What has been described as the basic mechanism of depression, the ego's shocking awareness of its helplessness in regard to its aspirations, is assumed to represent the core of normal, neurotic and probably psychotic depressions.... According to the viewpoint adopted here, depression represents a basic reaction to situations of narcissistic frustration which to prevent appears to be beyond the powers of the ego.[55]

Emotionally disturbed adolescents feel stronger needs for parental imposition of external controls and for conformity than do non-disturbed adolescents. Spivack hypothesizes that rebellious behaviour may be less characteristic of emotionally disturbed than of normal adolescents, which implies that the absence of rebellion may sometimes indicate emotional disturbance in young people.[56]

Holden shares the isolation of the traditional American hero. For him the society remains what it has always been for American heroes—an anti-community where the sense of materialism produces a pervasive deadening effect. One thinks of Sylvia Plath's *The Bell Jar,* whose heroine finds a correlative to the terror of inner emptiness in the social sterility of Madison Avenue glamour-just that world which Holden imagines himself as headed for. *The Man in the Grey Flannel Suit* and Sincerely, *Willis Wayde* too depict the world-weary cliches of growing up. The protagonists of these novels share with Holden an inability to conceptualize the future as anything but a dead end. "It didn't seem like anything was coming" (118) says Holden out of desperation.

D.M. Winnicott stresses the value of isolation to the adolescent: "Preservation of personal isolation is part of the search for identity and for the establishment of a personal technique for communicating which does not lead to violation of the central self."[57] The difficulty for Holden is that his culture offers no support for his struggle. The adults around him treat the problem like a headache as his mother does.

Holden struggles for moral purity in a corrupted American society. Unlike nineteenth-century characters, he wants to live in the society he belongs to, though with some reforms. While earlier American heroes like Hester Prynne and Huck Finn evaded social reality at the cost of denying their human need for others. Holden longs for everybody. In his own home, when he thinks about his father's profession, he knows that people go for money cannot save the innocent. But even if you were such an idealistic fellow, "how would you know if you did it because you really wanted to save guys' lives, or because what you really wanted to do was be a terrific lawyer, with everybody slapping you on the back and congratulating you in court..." (155).

Holden finds no such adult around him who can become a source of social strength for him to struggle toward maturity. Mr. Spencer, the history teacher who takes a fatherly interest in him, is actually interested in humiliating him. D.B., his older brother, is an emotionally remote from him as is his father. His mother, as he repeatedly notes, is too nervous and anxious herself to do more than pay perfunctory attention to her children's needs. There are no adults as moral tutors around Holden. Perhaps, as David Riesman puts it in speaking of middle-class American parents, "they are passing on to him their own contagious, highly diffuse anxiety," as they look to others to define values and goals increasingly based upon socially approved ephemera.[58]

In guiding adolescents, the characteristics and the development tasks which they hope to accomplish must be considered. Aware of their eagerness to achieve independence and their concern about developing their own philosophy of life, adults must share with them, informally and warmly, their own philosophy and perspective on life, their own values and standards. The adolescents must grow in self-understanding, in understanding how other people are feeling when they behave in certain ways, in capacities and values, and in the techniques of living. Thus the adolescent will develop "the maturity and flexibility to solve new problems as they are pesented."[59]

Parental attitudes and behaviour may either hinder or facilitate the child's achievement of maturity. The possessive and overprotective parent makes emancipation extremely difficult. The dominating parent may prevent an adolescent from benefiting from the new positive relations with his peers which are so important in achieving emancipation. The understanding parent helps with problems the adolescent cannot solve himself and also encourages him to be independent and to assume responsibilities he can carry. According to Mary Ellen Chase, many of the strained relationships between parents and older adolescents are owing to fear. "Parents fear that they may be unable to adjust to the new ideas, new speech, new manners and morals that their young people bring back from college or work; the young people fear that they may not be accepted again—may not be able to get back into the old friendly relationship."[60]

Fear and anxiety wreak their havoc, not only in such psychological manifestations as dread, apprehension and feelings of tension, but also in the form of physical illness. Kagan and Moss find evidence for suggesting that the early years of school-going appear to be a sensitive period in personality development. The more enduring traits—those that continue in adulthood—become manifest from adult six years of age to ten.[61] Kagan and Moss found that the degree of continuity of behaviours depends upon whether the behaviours were in accord with social norms. If they were they tended to persist; if not, they slowly changed.[62]

When after having a fight with Stradlater, Holden goes to Ackley's room for companionship, he finds him much more dirty than Stradlater. He finds his room stinking of his dirty socks. "You could hear old Ackley snoring.... That guy had just about everything. Sinus trouble, pimples, lousy teeth, halitosis, crumby fingernails. You had to feel a little sorry for the crazy sonuvabitch" (16). He once again feels very lonely and despair descends upon him. "I felt so lonesome, all of sudden, I almost wished I was dead.... Boy, did I feel rotten. I felt so damn lonesome" (42).

With his alienation go assorted hatreds—of the movies, of night clubs, of social and intellectual pretension, and so on. And physical disgust: pimples, sex, an old man picking his nose—all equally cause nausea to him. The narrative of the adolescent revolt in the following passage is worth quoting:

> When I was all set to go, when I had bags and all, I stood for a while next to the stairs and took a last look down the goddam corridor. I was sort of crying. I don't know why. I put my red hunting cap on, and turned the peak around to the back, the way I liked it, and then yelled at the top of my goddam voice, "Sleep tight, ya morons!" I'll bet I woke up every bastard on the whole floor. Then I got the hell out. Some stupid guy had thrown peanut shell all over the stairs, and I damn near broke my neck. (46)

Holden is obsessed by sickness, old age and death. His mind has been filled by the images of rot and decay. It is this obsessive concern of Holden's which accounts for the concentration of his narrative upon details of bodily functioning, dirt, and decay—filthy fingernails, mossy teeth, smelly socks, a rusty, filthy razor etc. When he meets his teachers, Mr. Spencer, besides his being "old," he hates his rotting bathrobe. In his form he finds sickness and old age:

> The minute I went in, I was sort of sorry I'd come. He was reading the *Atlantic Monthly*, and there were pills and medicines all over the place, and everything smelled of Vicks Nose Drops. It was pretty depressing. I'm not too crazy about sick people, anyway. What made it even more depressing, old Spencer had on this very sad, ratty old bathrobe that he was probably born in or something. I don't much like to see old guys in their pajamas and bathrobes anyway. Their bumpy old chests are always showing. And their legs. Old guy's legs, at beaches and places, always look so white and unhairy. (6)

He informs us that he did not know that the hotel, where he was staying was "full of perverts and morons...screwballs all over the place." What he sees in the hotel from the window of his room describes two scenes. In the first, a "distinguished looking man" is putting on "women's clothes—stockings, high heeled shoes,...walks in the room like a woman with small steps...smiling a cigarette and looking at himself in the mirror" (55). In the other room he sees "a man and a woman squirting water at each other in turns." And, in the morning, Holden tells us, "they were the highest of modesty." His indictment is overt in the following statement: "I was probably the only normal bastard in the whole place" (55).

This perversion is not confined to the hotel rooms only. Public places like museums, lavatories and even the walls of children's school are not save of this disgrace. "Fuck you" represents the final indignity that society can inflict upon mummies and innocent children and things Holden values. He laments, "It's hopeless...if you had a million years to do it in, you couldn't rub out even half the 'fuck you' signs in the world" (182). In disgust he says:

> ...you can't ever find a place that's nice and peaceful, because there isn't any. You may think there is, but once you get there, when you're not looking, somebody'll sneak up and write 'fuck you' right under your nose. Try it sometime. I think, even if I ever die, and they stick me in a cemetery and I have a tomb stone and all, it'll say, 'Holden Caulfield' on it, and then what year I was born and what year I died, and then right under that it'll say 'Fuck you.' (183)

Perhaps that is why the mummies in the museum have a considerable fascination for Holden as a realm of stillness, purity, and peace. More than once he wishes he were dead, like his brother Allie. There is bizarre fantasy of self and universal destruction. He wishes for death. He says "they'd better just take me out and stick me in front of a firing squad.... I'm sort of glad they've got the atomic bomb invented. If there's another war, I'm going to sit right the hell top of it. I'll volunteer for it, I swear to God I will." Because of the phoniness all round perhaps, he finds solace and comfort in the Museum of Natural History:

> The best thing, though, in that museum was that everything always stayed right where it was. Nobody'd move. You could go there a hundred thousand times, and that Eskimo would still be just finished catching these two fish, the bird would still be on their way south, the deers would still be drinking out of that water hole, with their pretty antlers and their pretty, skinny legs, and that squaw with the naked bosom would still be weaving that some blanket. Nobody'd be different (157-58). But there too, he finds the obscene words written with a red crayon or something right under the glass part of the wall, under the stones. (109)

In short, wherever he turns, he is frustrated by the phoniness of the world. Even the teachers are portrayed as sentimentalists and guardians of an exploded ethic: and one of them, Antolini, is a linguistic phony. He explains to Holden that the fall he is riding for is "a special kind of fall, a horrible kind. The man falling isn't permitted to feel or hear himself hit bottom. He just keeps falling and falling. The whole arrangement's designed for men who, at some time or other in their lives, were looking for something their own environment couldn't supply them with. Or they thought their own environment couldn't supply them with. So they gave up looking" (169). Mr. Antolini wants Holden to continue to search humanity for a cause worth living for. But whatsoever consolation it had, it is taken as an act of betrayal by the supposedly protective catcher. Though J.D. Salinger leaves the whole thing ambiguous, Peter J. Seng opines that "while there can be little doubt in a reader's mind about Antolini's propensities, his gesture toward Holden is considerably short of explicit."[63] Whatsoever it was, it leaves Holden disturbed.

Holden's disturbance is taken to be the fault of a hypocritical, uncaring society, particularly indifferent to its more sensitive souls. But Allie's death can also be accounted for much of Holden's abnormal mental state. Words like 'crazy,' 'mad,' 'madmen' and 'insane' have been frequently used in the novel. It is a matter of common knowledge that a single experience may change one's whole attitude towards life, and make a complete change in the character. Bitterness of character may be produced by a disappointment; a sexual assault may produce hysteria or sexual frigidity. Secondly, in childhood one is unadapted to life, and fails to react adequately to it. The death of someone near and dear is an irreparable loss and irretrievable disaster to a child; later, he learns to react to such exigencies of fate, and can meet them with greater composure and self-confidence. The childhood atmosphere determines whether the later attitude to the world be pessimistic, confident, stoical or antagonistic. Most of the psychotherapists hold the view that abnormal experiences of childhood, whether due to a single event or to an unnatural atmosphere, may have no immediate ill-effect, yet the impression is made, and the complex produced lies latent until later in life, when some shock or strain insufficient in itself to produce a neurosis, becomes active and there is a moral or nervous breakdown. "The adolescent," writes Peter Blos in *On Adolescence: A Psychoanalytic Interpretation*, "incurs a real loss in the renunciation of his oedipal parents, and he experiences the inner emptiness, grief, and sadness which is part of all mourning."[64] As E.H. Miller argues, *The Catcher in the Rye* is about Holden's need "to bury Allie before he can make the transition, to adulthood."[65] Since the child's personality is immature, it is not fully organized to cope with the unresolved problems of the childhood. Such problems relate mainly to matters of insecurity and fear and if the child does not receive necessary help and sense of security, it falls victim to fears and distress of all kinds.

The depressed adolescent's feeling of abandonment and unworthiness often leads him to turn away from rather than toward, people. The depressed adolescent often shuns people primarily to avoid being reminded that he feels abandoned and rejected by them. Lorand feels that "the painful psychic achievement of the adolescent—his detachment from parental authority—is so painful precisely because he experiences it not as a behaviour but as an abandonment by those objects on whom he relies for guidance and support. Hence, the reluctance sets in, accompanied by feelings of aloneness, emptiness, and helplessness, and a resentment towards the idea of abandoning the past."[66]

But finally, there is a will to live in the face of all horrors and failures. There is a will to survive in a confusing, irritating, and even sharply painful world. He emerges out of his depression to see a small child escaping danger and feels inspired by the poem he was singing:

> The kid was swell. He was walking in the street, instead of on the sidewalk, but right next to the curb. He was making out like he was walking on a very straight line, the way kids do, and the whole time he kept singing and humming. I got up closer so I could hear what he was singing. He was singing that song, "If a body catch a body coming through the rye." He had a pretty little voice, too. He was just singing for the hell of it, you could tell. The cars zoomed by, brakes screeched all over the place, his parents paid no attention to him, and he kept on walking next to the curb and singing.... (104)

Several critics have taken the last chapter as an ironic commentary on Holden's final helplessness, in the face of modernism and phoniness. Some critics arrive at a remarkably happy agreement about Holden's surrender to the forces of evil in American society. Charles Kaplan writes, "Ironically, he is revealed as telling us his narrative from an institution of some kind—psychiatric, we are led to suspect—having also been trapped by the people who want to 'sivilize' him."[67]

Soviet critics too agree with the fact that this book is about modern American life and the world around Holden which is dreary and spiritually bankrupt. Georgi Vladimov says that "Holden feels that he is the only sane being among psychopaths and living corpses.... Holden's only unfailing attachment is little children...."[68] Salinger feels that American society imposes its values on its individual members. At the close of the novel the gap between society and the individual widens and it reflects the American life lacking intellectual substance. A society that ignores or rejects Holden's gesture for understanding. "Supremely ironical, then, is our last glimpse of Holden making recovery and adjustment in the sanitarium—a prelude to compromise in the outside world.... Modern therapy takes over Holden's will to return. For Holden's sake we wouldn't have it otherwise, even though it's a return to the big money and dopey newsreels."[69]

Holden vainly attempts to break through the wall of phoniness in American society achieve love and community. At the end of the novel he says: "About all I know is, I sort of miss everything I told about. Even old Stradlater and Ackley, for instance. I think I even miss that goddam Maurice." Critics opine that Holden remains a confirmed isolate at the end of the book. Alfred Kazin includes Holden in the sweeping pronouncement that "in Salinger's work the two estates—the world and the cutely sensitive young—never really touch at all."[70] Peter J. Seng, otherwise perceptive in nothing Holden's obvious incapacity to act as an arbiter of moral values in an adult society, insists that Holden at the end is the tragic author of his own undoing. Holden's "flaw" resides in "a naive refusal to come to terms with the world in which he lives."[71]

But Holden is not, as many of Salinger's critics have maintained, a tragic figure, a victim of modern society. He is not defeated at the end, and he has come to terms with the world in which he must live. There is a juxtaposition of the sacred and the profane. As Ihab Hassan has stressed, "Revulsion and holiness make up the rack on which Salinger's art twitches."[72] His character development is all about how to remain innocent, truthful amidst the obscene and corrupt world. The conclusion is a positive one, showing "how exposure of the sensitive soul to the darkness of this present age can lead not only to sickness but also to healing."[73]

NOTES AND REFERENCES

1. Irene M. Josselyn, *The Adolescent and His World*, New York: Family Service Association of America, 1952, 16.
2. Erik H. Erikson, "Childhood and Society," *Identity: Youth and Crisis* (New York: Norton, 1968).
3. C.J. Jung, "The Archetypes of the Collective Unconscious," *The Collected Works of C.J. Jung Herbert Read* Vol. VII (New York: Pantheon Books, Bollingen Series XX, 1966) 110.
4. Peter and Jane Davison, "Coming of Age in America" *New York Times Magazine*, 1975.
5. *The Poetical Works of John Keats*, ed. Buxton Forman (London, 1946) 56.

6. Arthur L. Stinchombe, *Rebellion in a High School* (Chicago: Quadrangle Books, 1964) 5-6.
7. L.F. Cervantes, *The Dropout: Causes and Cures* (Ann Arbor: University of Michigan P, 1965) 192.
8. J.G. Bachman, Green, S. & Wirtanen, I. *Dropping Out—Problem or Symptom* (Ann Arbor: Institute for Social Research, University of Michigan P, 1967) 29.
9. L.F. Cervantes, *The Dropout: Causes and Cures* (Ann Arbor: University of Michigan P, 1965) 192-93.
10. S.M. Finch, *Fundamental of Child Psychiatry* (New York: Norton, 1960) 309-10.
11. H. Wilson, The early diagnosis of schizophrenia, *British Medical Journal*, 1: 1502-04.
12. William Wiegand, "J.D. Salinger: Seventy-Eight Bannanas," *Chicago Review*, IX (Winter 1958) 3-19.
13. R.J. Havighurst, and H. Taba, *Adolescent Character and Personality*, Published by John Wiley & Sons, Inc., 1949, 95.
14. Ernest J. Chave, *Personality Development in Children* (Chicago: University of Chicago P, 1937) 202-03.
15. *Ibid.* 221.
16. L.S. Feuer, *The Conflict of Generations* (New York: Basic Books, 1969).
17. Henry A. Murray, "Time for a Positive Morality," *Survey Graphic*, 36: 195-96, 214-16 (1947).
18. Kenneth, Keniston, *The Uncommitted: Alienated Youth in American Society* (New York: Dell, 1960).
19. *Ibid.* 394.
20. L.N. Robins, Chapter In: Quay, H.C. and Warry J.S. (Eds.) *Psychopathological Disorders of Childhood* (London: Wiley, 1972).
21. Nash K. Burger, A review in *The Times*.
22. Arthur Heiserman and James E. Miller, Jr., "J.D. Salinger: Some Crazy Cliff," *Western Humanities Review*, X (Spring 1956) 129-37.
23. Endicott Peabody, "The Continuous Moral Influence of the School Through College and Life," *School Review* 7 (1899) 627-28.
24. *Youth: Transition to Adulthood. Report of the Panel on Youth of the President's Science Advisory Committee* (Washington, D.C.: U.S. Government Printing Office, 1973) 125.
25. Devid Riesman, *The Lonely Crowd: A Study of the Changing American Character* (New Haven: Yale University Press, rev. ed. 1970) 5.
26. James E. Bryan discusses the issue through "clinical approach" in his article "The Psychological Structure of *The Catcher in the Rye*," *PMLA* Vol. 89, No. 5 (October 1974) 1065-74.
27. Crow & Crow, *Adolescent development and adjustment*, McGraw-Hill Book Company, Inc., New York, 1951.

28. Robert Havighurst, "Poised at the Cross roads of Life; Suggestions to Parents and Teachers of Young Adolescents," *School Review*, Vol. 61 (September 1953) 329-36.
29. Harvey Breit, *The Atlantic* 189 (August 1951) 82.
30. S.N. Behrman, "The Vision of the Innocent," *The New Yorker* (August 11, 1951) 71.
31. Brain Way, "'Franny and Zooey' and J.D. Salinger," *New Left Review*, May-June 1962, 72-82.
32. *Ibid.*
33. L. Kohlberg, A Cognitive-developmental analysis of children's sex-role concepts and attitudes. In E.E. Maccoby (Ed.), *The development of sex-differences*, Stanford UP, 1966, 82-173.
34. I.B. Weiner, *Psychological Disturbances in Adolescence*, John Wiley, New York, 1970.
35. N.W. Ackerman, 'Adolescent Problems: a symptom of family disorder,' *Family Process*, 1, 1962, 202-13.
36. Donald P. Costello, 'The Language of The Catcher in the Rye,' *American Speech*, XXXIV (October 1959).
37. Donald Barr, 'Saints, Pilgrims, and Artists,' *Commonweal, LXVII* (October 25, 1957) 90.
38. Arthur Heiserman and James E. Miller, Jr., 'J.D. Salinger: Some Crazy Cliff,' *Western Humanities Review*, X (1956) 136.
39. S.N. Behrman, 'The Vision of the Innocent,' *New Yorker*, XXVII (August 11, 1951) 72.
40. Carl F. Strauch, 'Kings in the Back Row: Meaning Through Structure,' A Reading of Salinger's *The Catcher in the Rye, Wisconsin Studies in Contemporary Literature*, II (Winter, 1961) 5-30.
41. Edward P.J. Corbett, "Raise High the Barriers, Censors," in *J.D. Salinger and the Critics* 55.
42. David L. Stevenson, "D.D. Salinger: The Mirror of Crisis," *The Nation* (March 1959) 215.
43. Arthur Mizener, "The Love Song of J.D. Salinger", *Harper's* (February 1959) 87.
44. Carol and Richard Ohmann, "Reviews, Critics and Catcher," *Critical Inquiry* (Autumn, 1976) 35.
45. Maxwell Gismar, *American Moderns: From Rebellion to Conformity*, (New York: Hill and Wang, Inc. 1958) 198.
46. James E. Bryan, "The Psychological Structure of The Catcher in the Rye," *PMLA*, Vol. 89, No. 5 (1973) 1065-74.
47. Charles H. Kegel, "Incommunicability in Salinger's *The Catcher in the Rye*," *The Western Humanities Review*, XI (Spring, 1957) 188-90.
48. Peter J. Seng, "The Fallen Idol: The Immature World of Holden Caulfield," *College English* 23 (December 1961) 208.

49. William Wiegand, "J.D. Salinger: Seventy-Eight Bannanas," *Chicago Review*, IX (Winter 1958).

50. Keniston K., *The Uncommitted: Alienated Youth in American Society* (New York: Dell, 1960) 454.

51. *Ibid.* 465.

52. J.S. Coleman, *The Adolescent Society* (New York: Free Press of Glencoe, 1961) 3.

53. J.S. Coleman, "The Adolescent Subculture and Academic Achievement," *American Journal of Sociology*, 65: 337-47, 1960.

54. Konopka. See for ref. book by Rogers, 125.

55. E. Birbriny, "The mechanism of depression," in P. Greenacre, ed., *Affective Disorders* (New York: International UP, 1953) 13-48.

56. G. Spivack, Child-rearing attitudes of emotionally disturbed adolescents. *Journal of Consulting Psychology*, 21: 178, 1957.

57. D.W. Winnicott, *The Maturational Process and the Facilitating Environment* (New York: The International Universities P, 1965), 190.

58. David Riesman, *The Lonely Crowds: A Study of the Changing American Character* (New Haven: Yale UP, 1950) 49.

59. Gardner Murphy, "The Cultural Context of Guidance," *Personnel and Guidance Journal*, Vol. 34 (September 1955) 8.

60. Mary Ellen Chase, "When You Go Home," *Coronet*, Vol. 33 (December 1952) 23-27.

61. Kagan, J. and Moss, H.A., "Birth to Maturity: A Study in Psychological Development." New York: Wiley, 962.

62. Kagan J. and Moss, H.A., "The Stability of Passive and dependent behaviour from childhood through adulthood." *Child Development*, 31, 577-91.

63. Peter J. Seng, "The Fallen Idol: the Immature World of Holden Caulfield," *College English*, 23 (December 1961) 208.

64. Peter Blos, *On Adolescence: A Psychoanalytic Interpretation* (New York: The Free Press, 1962) 100.

65. E.H. Miller, "In Memoriam: Allie Caulfield in *The Catcher in the Rye*." *Mosaic: A Journal for the Interdisciplinary Study of Literature* 15 (Winter, 1982) 129.

66. S. Lorand, "Adolescent Depression," *International Journal of Psycho-Analysis*, 48: 53-60, 1967.

67. Charles Kaplan, "Holden and Huck: The Odysseys of Youth," *College English*, XVIII (November 1956) 78.

68. Chugunov Konstantin, Soviet Critics on J.D. Salinger's Novel, *The Catcher in the Rye, Soviet Literature*, No. 5, 1962, 182-84.

69. Branch, *op. cit.*, 156.

70. J.D. Salinger, "Everybody's Favourite," reprinted in *Contemporaries*, Boston, 1962, 238.

71. Peter J. Seng, "The Fallen Idol: The Immature World of Holden Caulfield," *College English*, XXIII, December 1961, 209.
72. Ihab Hassan, *Radical Innocence: Studies in the Contemporary American Novel* (Princeton: Princeton UP, 1961) 288.
73. Kenneth Hamilton, *J.D. Salinger: A Critical Essay* (Grand Rapids, Mich: Eerdmans, 1967) 39.

5

CONCLUSION

The novels and stories I have discussed, despite the isolation, nausea, anxiety and despair which the protagonists experience, end not on a note of cynical despair but regeneration and hope. The young protagonists suffer from a general incapacity to adjust with the environment—psychic, physical or moral. No longer motivated by love, ambition or money, they respond to unconscious feelings of guilt, domestic frustration, and the hangovers of insecurity in infancy.

Though powerless to act, the young protagonist cannot help struggling desperately to know himself. This condition of being a no-man, exposes him to the terrifying vision of nothingness. Engaged in an obsessive search for the self, he is at war not only with society but also with himself. His personality splits and disintegrates a number of times. Too weak to encounter the absurdity of existence, he becomes a victim of psychological tensions. He is also projected as a victim demonstrating all the symptoms of a moral and spiritual fragmentation, alienation, nausea and despair. And the cause of all this is not man's relationship with the universe, but the social environment.

The literature of 1920's is mainly about the failure of culture, entertainment, family life, religion, material success and spiritual failure. The generation who took over in the post-war decade could have little confidence in the percepts of their country. There was a mood of rejection all around, abundantly supported by an accumulation of prejudices and views. The emotional and aesthetic needs of the younger generation were adversely affected by the failure of communication, morality, social meaning and value. Faith in the older generation and their traditions was shaken badly. Stability and convention were condemned because all evidences of stability seemed illusory and artificial. There was a marked disrespect for tradition amongst the youngsters. The war had shattered their illusions and the young generation had every right to reject the traditions.

The later collection of Miranda Stories—"Old Mortality" and "Pale Horse, Pale Rider"—reveal the pressures of the circumstances and the state of no choice. The story "Pale Horse, Pale Rider" is particularly imbued with a peculiar atmosphere which permeated the United States during World War I with its perverse sense of patriotism, its distorted vision of the enemy, its sometimes brutal pressures for conformity. Here Ms. Porter allows a completely subjective confrontation of situation within her heroine's consciousness symbolizing Miranda's determination to remain loyal to her own convictions. She cannot accept the traditions of the older generations. She must find her own terms. In her stories Ms. Porter has described the new sexual morality and the modified roles of the woman. She has also discussed many other social, political and cultural developments which have profoundly affected the adolescent experience in the United States. In her early stories published in the twenties and thirties the young women are in conflict with socially-imposed rules. The stories written in the period 1929-30 reveal a level of psychological conflict. Reaching against humanistic, psychological or aesthetic theories, the adolescent is trapped by necessity and engulfed by spiritual gloom. The new sense of uncertainty, anxiety and pessimism resulted in decay, fragmentation, alienation, anguish and morbidity.

Katherine Anne Porter's later stories and J.D. Salinger's *The Catcher in the Rye* most appropriately suggest the modern predicament of alienation, the estrangement or aloneness of an individual within his own group. These novelists deal with those attitudes that are basic to the American view of life. The analysis of the novels demonstrates that since the contemporary protagonists suffer from identity crisis, their quest for objective truth is based on illusion—an attitude antithetical to the mythical heroes. Feeling isolated the hero distrusts truth, justice and love, and negates everything conforming to a value-oriented society. No wonder, instead of emerging as a saviour, the adolescent hero is seen as a destroyer. Conceived under the influence of Freudian and neo-Freudian theories, the modern protagonist is essentially a disintegrated self, too weak to confront existence.

The individual in Ms. Porter's works desires to understand the past, and compares it to the failures of modern man in a mechanized, chaotic world. She herself believed in an ancient system of ethics, unanswerable, indispensable moral law. The source and strength of stories like "Old Mortality" lies in what Stewart call, "Recognition of the two kinds, the legendary and the actual...."[1] Ms. Porter's aim is to bring out the tension between the legend and the reality. Miranda's nostalgia at the disintegration of the country house and the disappearance of the family seat are a delusion as well as ideal. In this barbaric age, Ms. Porter longs for the pastoral world of the past but mocks its inadequacy to meet the contemporary challenges.

This paradox of delusion is essential to her art and philosophy of life. Her work is an amalgam of the traditional and the modern, an amalgam of alienation with traditional prejudices, of an unviable marriage between institutions, values and two different epochs. Her main interest lay in probing the depths of human emotions as well analysing the outward appearance of social conventions and human behaviour. She feels that she must portray the actual world by juxtaposing fantasy with reality, tradition with modernity, so that the contrast would heighten the grim sense of contemporary reality. From the tensions of differing truths and angry confusion, arising out of the conflict between inhibition and impulse, she evolves her rich social vision.

J.D. Salinger is not as much obsessed by traditionalism as by the violation of this traditional order by forces of modernity and instability. The contrast in his vision of a bygone historical world of certainty and order and the declining and decaying present civilization brings out the sharpening of social conflict. David Lodge feels that when culture is seen as a process of decline, "...nothing is invulnerable to irony. The modern is ridiculed by contrast with the traditional, but attempts to maintain or restore the traditional in the face of change are also seen as ridiculous; and in any case the traditional usually turns out to be in some way false or compromised."[2]

Hurrocks comments that American adolescents of today are different from those of past generations and from other societies not because of alterations in hereditary endowment but because of cultural differences.[3] Stone and Church conclude from inter-social variations in adolescent behaviour patterns that "the individual psychology of adolescence can only be grasped against the sociology and social psychology of the age."[4]

J.D. Salinger moves into his strongly modernized world in which human figures are distorted and strangely weary of life. The young protagonist in his novel is in trouble while coping with the postwar world in which "disorder seems notably prevalent, value historically extracted, chaos come again as a direct result of the war and its disorientation and dehumanization."[5] Transitory experience, instability of identity and society and divided natures become the habitual components of Salinger's writings.

The period after the wars is regarded as one of protest, frustration, social violence, riots, radical changes in life styles, the widespread rejection of traditional American values, the breaking down of established behavioural patterns and loss of faith in the present system. The young people who had confronted this violence, were expected somehow to bring these factors in line with the traditional moral and ethical ideas taught in their schools, their churches and in their homes. But it was not easy for the youngsters, instead they showed their distrust in traditional values. The attitudes and thoughts of Zen Budhism attracted many young people. According to Tanner and Bryant, "the predominant thematic emphasis of this literary period was on anti-authoritarianism, and anti-materialism, deeply concerned with the clash between the idealistic hero and the corrupt society which surrounds him, puzzled over the question of what constitutes reality, and confused as to the proper balance between the right to individual freedom and the necessary constraints of society."[6] Both of these critics see American literature after the World Wars as portraying a central character uncertain of his identity, usually at odds with the values of society.

The twentieth century has been widely described in literature, as well as in the writings of modern philosophers, sociologists and psychologists as "an age of anxiety."[7] The general consensus is that the age is characterised by emptiness and loss of meaning. The break-down of religion has contributed to the experience of the age by depriving modern man a frame of orientation and a feeling of security. Individuals and society have always been in a state of uncomfortable relationship. Social epochs have, by and large, demanded the individual's conformity, while individuals have either rebelled against social constraints or willingly accepted them. Salinger's *The Catcher in the Rye* very aptly articulates this uneasy relationship. Indeed the novel has projected this relationship beautifully. Here the individual is fighting at two fronts: against his isolation and against the society. Recent studies of the term alienation, assign philosophical, psychological, sociological and political connotations to it. With modern society undergoing vast and rapid change and with the crumbling of traditional patterns of relationships, an individual feels adrift, alone and frustrated. Helen Merrell Lynd makes a profound observation when characterising the main attributes of the contemporary period of history, which according to her, is called,

> ...a new period of failure of nerve, an age of conformity, a period of anomie or cultural chaos, of escape from freedom, a new age of treason, an age of longing, a decline of the West. Much is heard of the dilemma of liberalism, the distrust of the democratic process, the revolt of the masses, the failure of self-determination, the loss of command over the environment. We who live in this age are described as alienated, estranged, isolated, alone, a lost generation depersonalized, other-directed double men.[8]

Alienation being an inevitable phenomenon in modern society, it is but natural that the hero in Salinger's novel should experience it. Salinger's main concern is with the dehumanizing effects of urbanization and technological developments on the psyche of an individual. An incessant striving for wealth, luxuries and comforts of technological civilization lead the individual to spiritual vacuity. He feels, as does Norman Mailer that "life in America becomes more economically prosperous and more psychically impoverished each year. The individual captivated by the affluence of the industrialized society is finally mutilated into a machine."[9]

The hero who conforms to the dehumanized urban and industrial environment, is alienated from his psyche and from the abiding values of life. The corrupting material environment dehumanizes society. The description of a night in New York, by Holden is quite nightmarish:

> ...It was so quiet and lonesome out, even though it was Saturday night. I didn't see hardly anybody on the street.... Now and then you just saw a man and a girl crossing a street, with their arms around each other's waists and all, or a bunch of hoodlumy—looking guys and their dates, all of them laughing like hyenas at something you could just bet wasn't funny. New York's terrible one somebody laughs on the street very late at night. You can hear it for miles. It makes you feel so lonesome and depressed. I kept wishing I could go home. (74)

This is a picture of emptiness, reflecting the spiritual isolation of the persons who inhabit such streets. Their nihilism is intensified and their alienation from society accentuated. David Reisman, the sociologist, considers isolation to be a "recent phenomenon."[10] He attributes it to the rapid industrialization of society in which each man lacking in self-sufficiency fears that he would be ridiculed if he is different from the crowd, hence he spends all his effort to conform to the social norms. In this process he not only gets separated from himself but also from the crowd which is as lonely as he, and with whom his communication is no deeper than the surface level.

It is in Salinger's single novel, *The Catcher in the Rye*, that the period finds its testament of loss. Humour, irony, and wistfulness barely conceal the sadness of city life, the equivocations of society, the reign of solitude. The novel mocks of hypocrisy, egoism, compromise, and also comes close to sounding the note of dread. But Holden, the hero of the novel, though he can love only his sister Phoebe, retains the saving grace of vulnerability.

J.D. Salinger and Katherine Anne Porter both depict the adolescent as innocent, confused, frustrated and disillusioned, who in the innocence of childhood is afraid of growing up. There is a tone of hoplessness as well as a suggestion of freedom from the relentless determinism of the past. The awakenings of the adolescence permit new resolutions to old conflicts.

NOTES AND REFERENCES

1. John L. Stewart, *The Burden of Time: The Fugitives and Agrarians* (Princeton UP, 1965) 96.
2. David Lodge, "Evelyn Waugh" in Columbia Essays on Modern Writers (New York: 1971) 8-10.
3. J.E. Hurrocks, *The Psychology of Adolescence*, 2nd Edition (Boston: Houghton-Miffin, 1962) 6.
4. L.J. Stone and J. Church, *Childhood and Adolescence*, 2nd Edition (New York: Random House, 1968) 438.
5. Malcolm Brodhury, *Possibilities: Essays on the State of the Novel* (London: OUP, 1973) 144.
6. Tony Tanner, *City of Words: American Fiction 1950-1970*. The Free Press, 1970.
7. Paul Iillich, *The Courage To Be* (London: Collins, 1952) 48.
8. Helen Merrell Lynd, *On Shame and the Search for Identity* (New York: Harcourt, Brace & Co., 1958) 15.
9. Norman Mailer, *Advertisements for Myself* (New York: G.P. Putnam's Sons, 1959) 414-23.
10. David Riesman, *The Lonely Crowd: A Study of the Changing American Character* (New Haven: Yale UP, 1950).

Bibliography

Primary Sources

Porter, Katherine Anne. *The Collected Essays and Occasional Writings of Katherine Anne Porter.* New York: Delaocorte Press, 1970.

——. *Collected Stories of Katherine Anne Porter.* New York: Harcourt, Brace and World, Inc., 1965.

——. *The Days Before.* New York: Harcourt, Brace and Co., 1952.

——. *Flowering Judas and Other Stories.* New York: The Modern Library, 1940.

——. "Introduction: *Selected Stories of Eudora Welty.* New York: Random House, 1943.

——. *Pale Horse, Pale Rider: Three Short Novels.* New York: Harcourt, Brace and Company, 1942.

Salinger, Jerome David. *The Catcher in the Rye.* New York: Penguin Books, 1951. All page numbers are from this edition.

Secondary Sources

Ackerman, N.W. 'Adolescent Problems: A Symptom of Family Disorder.' *Family Process,* 1: 202-13, 1962.

Adam, Jane. *The Spirit of Youth and the City Streets.* New York: Macmillan, 1910.

Ausubel, D. & H. Schiff. "Some Intrapersonal and Interpersonal Determinants of Individuals Differences in Socio-empathic Ability Among Adolescents," *Journal of Social Psychology.* 1955, 41, 39-56.

Bachman, J.G., Green, S. & Wirtanen, I. *Dropping Out—Problem or Symptom.* Ann Arbor: Institute for Social Research, University of Michigan, 1972.

Bebel, August. *Woman in the Past, Present and Future.* Trans. H.B. Adams Walthor (London: Modern Press, 1985).

Behrman, S.N. "The Vision of the Innocent." *The New Yorker* (August 11, 1951).

Belcher, William F. and James W. Lee, eds. *J.D. Salinger and the Critics.* Belmont, California: Wadsworth Publishing Co., 1962.

Ben, D.J. "Beliefs, attitudes and human affairs." Belmont, California: Wadsworth Publishing Co., 1970.

Bibriny, E. The Mechanism of Depression. In P. Greenacre, ed., *Affective Disorders.* New York: International University Press, 1953.

A Bibliography of the Works of Katherine Anne Porter and a Bibliography of the Criticism of the Works of Katherine Anne Porter. Ed. Louise Waldrip and Shirley Anne Bauer. New Jersey: Searecrow Press, Methehen, 1969.

Blos, P. 'The Second Individuation Process of Adolescence.' *Psychoanalytic Study of the Child*, 22.

Branch, Edgar. "Mark Twain and J.D. Salinger: A Study of Literary Continuity." *American Quarterly*, 9 (Summer 1957).

Breit, Harvey. "Reader's Choice." *The Atlantic* 189 (August 1951).

Brooks, Cleanth. "The Southern Temper" in *The Shaping Joy: Studies in the Writer's Craft.* London: Methuen and Co. Ltd., 1971.

Brooks, Van Wyck. *The Writer in America* (New York: Dutton, 1953).

Bryan, James D. "The Psychological Structure of *The Catcher in the Rye.*" *PMLA*, Vol. 89, No. 5 (1974) 1065-74.

Calhoun, Arthur W. *A Social History of the American Family: Colonial Period* (New York: Barnes and Noble, 1960, I. 132).

Carol and Richard Ohmann. "Reviews, Critics and Catcher." *Critical Enquiry* (Autumn, 1976) 35.

Carpenter, Frederic I. "Adolescent in American Fiction." *The English Journal.* XLVI (September 1957).

Cervantes, L.F. *The Drop Out: Causes and Cures* (Ann Arbor: University of Michigan P, 1965) 192.

Chase, Marry Ellen. "When you Gottome." *Coronet*, Vol. 33 (December 1952).

Chave, Ernest J. *Personality Development in Children*. Chicago: University of Chicago P, 1937.

Chugunov, Konstantin. "Soviet Critics on J.D. Salinger's Novel, *The Catcher in the Rye*." *Soviet Literature*, No. 5, 1962.

Cole, Luella. *Psychology of Adolescence*. 7th ed., Rinehart & Company, Inc., New York, 1959.

Coleman, J.S. *The Adolescent Society*. New York: Free Press of Glencoe, 1961.

Conger, J.J. "Adolescence: Generation Under Pressure." *Curacao The Life Cycle Serier Willemstad*, Multimedia Publications, Inc., 1979.

Cooper, D. *Death of the Family*. New York: Panthever, 1970.

Cooper, J.B. Parent evaluation as related to social ideology and academic achievement. *J. Genet. Psychol.*, 1962, 101, 135-43.

Corbett, Edward P.J. "Some Thoughts on *The Catcher in the Rye*; Raise High the Barriers, Censore." *America*, CIV (7 January 1961), 441-43.

Costello, Donald P. "The Language of *The Catcher in the Rye*." *American Speech*. XXXIV (October 1959).

Crow, L.D. and A. Crow. *Adolescent Development and Adjustment*. McGraw-Hill Book Company, Inc., New York, 1951.

Cruze, W.W. *Adolescent Psychology and Development*. The Ronald Press Company, New York, 1944.

Dallard, John, Leonard Doob, Neal E. Miller, O.H. Mowrer, and Robert R. Sears. *Frustration and Aggression*. New Haven: Yale UP, 1939.

Deutsch, Helen. "Selected Problems of adolescence with special emphasis on group formation." The Monograph series of the Psychoanalytic Study of the Child, Monograph No. 3; Hogarth Press and the Institute of Psycho Analysis, 1968.

Dingwall, Eric John. *The American Woman: A Historical Study*. London: Gerald Duckworth & Co. Ltd., 1956.

"The Divided Self: Jean Paul Sarte to R.D. Laing," in *Maps of the Mind.* ed. Charles Hampden Turner. New York: Mitchell Beazley, 1980.

Dovvan, E.A. & Adelson, J. *The adolescent experience.* New York: Willey, 1966, 85.

Ehrmann, Winston. "Changing Sexual Mores." *Values and Ideals of American Youth.* ed. Eli Ginzberg. New York: Columbia UP, 1964.

Eisinger, Chester. "Introduction: The Shape of the Forties." *Fiction of the Forties.* Chicago: University of Chicago P, 1963.

Elkind, D. Children and Adolescents. *Interpretative Essays on Jean Piaget.* New York: OUP, 1970.

Elizabeth Janeway, "Women's Literature." *Harvard Guide to Contemporary American Writing.* ed. Daniel Hoffman (Delhi: OUP, 1979).

Endicott Peabody. "The Continuous Moral Influence of the School Through College and Life." *School Review* 7 (1899) 627-28.

Erikson, E.H. *Identity: Youth and Crisis.* New York: Norton, 1968.

——. The problem of ego identity. *Journal of the American Psychoanalytic Association.* 1956, 4, 56-121.

——. *Childhood and Society.* New York: Norton, 1968.

Evans, R.J. Dialogue with Eric Harrison. New York: Harper & Row, 1967.

Faulkner, William. *Requiem For a Nun.* Middlesex: Penguin Books, 1970.

Feuer, L.S. *The Conflict of Generations.* New York: Basic Books, 1969.

Fiedler, Leslie A. "From Redemption to Initiation." *The New Leader.* XLI (26 May 1958).

Finch, S.M. *Fundamentals of Child Psychiatry.* New York: Norton, 1960.

French, Warren. *J.D. Salinger*. New York: Twayne, 1963.

Freud, A. *The Ego and the Mechanisms of Defense*. New York: International UP, 1936.

Freud, Sigmund. *Beyond the Pleasure Principal*. 1922.

Gallagher and Harris. *Emotional Problems of Adolescents*. New York: OUP, 1976.

Gardner, Murphy. "The Cultural Context of Guidance," *Personnel and Guidance Journal*. Vol. 34 (September 1955).

Geismar, Maxwell. "The American Short Story Today." *Studies on the Left*, 4 (Spring, 1964).

——. *American Moderns: From Rebellion to Conformity*. New York: Hill and Wang, Inc., 1958.

——. "Tragic *Versus* Comic America: Society and the Novel." *Modern American Literature*.

Gombrich, E.H, *Art and Illusion: A Study in the Psychology of Pictorial Representation*. Princeton: Princeton UP, 1960.

Gordan, Ira J. *Human Development—A Trans-sectional Perspective*. New York: Harper, 1962.

Grinder, Robert E. "Socialization: Adolescence and Society." *Studies in Adolescence*. New York: Macmillan, 1975.

Hall, G. Stanley. *Adolescence: Its Psychology and its Relations to Physiology, Anthropology, Sociology, Sex, Crime, Religion and Education*, Vol. I and II. New York: D. Appleton, 1904.

Hamilton, Kenneth. *J.D. Salinger: A Critical Essay*. Grand Rapids: William B. Eerdmans, 1967.

Hardy, John Edward. *Katherine Anne Porter*. New York: Fredrick Ungar Publishing Co., 1973.

Hartley, Lodwick. "Katherine Anne Porter." *Sewanee Review*, 48 (1940).

Hassan, Ihab H., "J.D. Salinger: Rare Quixotic Gesture." *Radical Innocence: Studies in the Contemporary American Novel*. New York: Harper & Row, 1961.

Havighurst, R.J. and H. Taba. *The Adolescent Character and Personality*. John Wiley & Sons, Inc., New York, 1949.

Havighurst, Robert. "Poised at the Crossroads of Life: Suggestions to Parents and Teachers of Young Adolescents." *School Review*, Vol. 61 (September 1953).

Heiserman, Arthur, and James E.Miller, Jr. "J.D. Salinger: Some Crazy Cliff." *Western Humanities Review*, X (Spring, 1956).

Hokman, C. Hugh. "The Rebirth of the South: Wolfe Faulkner, Warren," *Modern American Literature*.

Horton and Edwards. *Background of American Literary Thought*. New Jersey: Princeton Hall, Inc., 1974.

Hurrocks, J.E. *The Psychology of Adolescence*. 2nd Edition. Boston: Houghton-Miffin, 1962.

Iillich, Paul. *The Courage To Be* (London: Collins, 1952).

Johnson, James William. "Another Look at Katherine Anne Porter. *Virginia Quarterly Review*, 36 (Autumn, 1960).

——. "The Adolescent Hero: A Trend in Modern Fiction." *Twentieth Century Literature*, V (April 1959).

Johnson, Wendell. *People in Quandaries*. New York: Harper & Bros., 1964.

Josselyn, Irene M. *The Adolescent and His World*. New York: Family Service Association of America, 1952.

Jung, C.G. "The Archetypes of the Collective Unconscious," *The Collected Works of C.G. Jung*. Herbert Read (New York: Pantheon Books, Bollingen Series XX 1966) Vol. VII.

Kagan, J., and Moss, H.A. "The Stability of Passive and dependent behaviour from childhood through adulthood," *Child Development*, 31, 577-91.

——. *Birth to Maturity: A Study in Psychological Development*. New York: Wiley, 1962.

Kaplan, Charles. "Holden and Huck: The Odysseys of Youth." *College English*, XVIII (November 1956) 78.

Kegel, Charles H. "Incommunicability in Salinger's *The Catcher in the Rye*." *Western Humanities Review*, XI (Spring, 1957) 188-90.

Keniston, Kenneth. *The Uncommitted: Alienated Youth in American Society*, New York: Dell, 1960.

Keniston, Kenneth. *Young Radicals*. Harcourt, Brace & World. New York, 1968.

Kohlberg, L. A cognitive-developmental analysis of children's sex-role concepts and attitudes. In E.E. Maccoby (ed.) *The development of sex-differences*. Stanford Cal.: Stanford UP, 1966, 82-173.

Kohlberg, L. & Gilligan, C. "The adolescent as a philosopher: The discovery of the self in a post-conventional world." *Daedalus*, Fall, 1971, 1066-67.

Konopka, Gisela. "Requirements for Healthy Developments of Adolescent Youth." *Adolescence*, Fall, 1973.

Krishnamurthy, M.G. *Katherine Anne Porter: A Study*. Mysore: Rao and Raghvan, 1971.

Laser, Marvin and Norman Furman (eds.). *Studies in J.D. Salinger: Reviews, Essays and Critiques of the Catcher in the Rye and Other Fiction*. New York: Osyssey Press, 1963.

Lodge, David. "Ectyn Waugh" in *Columbia Essays on Modern Writers* (New York 1971).

Lorand, S. "Adolescent depression." *International Journal of Psycho-Analysis*, 48: 53-60, 1967.

Lorch, B.D. "The Perception of Deviancy of Self and Others," *Social and Social Research*, 50: 223-29, 1966.

Lowrie, Samuel H. Early Marriage: Premarital pregnancy and associated factors. *Journal of Marriage and the Family* 27 (February 1965) 53.

Lydall, Gorden. *Virginia Woolf: A Writer's Life*. Oxford: OUP, 1984) 256.

Lynd, Helen Merrell. *On Shame and the Search for Identity* (New York: Harcourt, Brace & Co., 1958).

Mannheim, Karl. *Essays on the Sociology of Culture*. New York: OUP, 1956.

Marcus, Mordecai. "What is an Initiation Story?" *Critical Approaches to Fiction*, ed. Shiv K. Kumar and Meith Mackean. New York: McGraw, 1968.

McCandless, B.R. *Adolescents: Behaviour and Development*. New York: Halt, Rinehart and Winston, 1971.

Mead, M. *Culture and Commitment: A Study of the Generation Gap*. Garden City, New York: Doubleday, 1970.

Miller, E.H. "In Memorium: Allie Caulfield in *The Catcher in the Rye*." *Mosaic*: A Journal for the Interdisciplinary Study of Literature 15 (Winter, 1982) 129.

Mitchell, J.V. Jr., "Goal-Setting Behaviour as a Function of Self-Acceptance over and underachievement, Related Personality Variables." *Journal of Educational Psychology*, 50: 93-104, 1959.

Mizener, Arthur. "The Love Song of J.S. Salinger." *Harper's* CCXVIII (February 1959) 83-90.

Murray, Henry, A. "Time for a Positive Morality." *Survey Graphic*, 36: 195-96, 214-16 (1947).

Musgrove, Frank. *Youth and the Social Order*. Bloomington, Ind.: Indiana UP, 1965.

Mussen, P.H., Conger, J.J., & Kagan, J. *Child Development and Personality*. New York: Harper & Row, 1969 (3rd ed.).

Nance, William L. *Katherine Anne Porter and the Art of Rejection*. Chapel Hill: University of North Carolina P, 1964.

Nixon, R. "Psychological Normality in the Years of Youth, *Teacher College Record*, 66: 71-74, 1964.

Outline of Mexican Popular Arts and Crafts. Los Angeles: Young & M. Callister, Inc., 1922.

Pearson, G.H.J. *Adolescence and the Conflict of Generations: An Introduction to some of the Psychoanalytic Contributions to the Understanding of Adolescence*. New York: W.W. Norton & Company, Inc., 1958.

Peter and Jane Davison. "Coming of Age in America." *New York Times Magazine*, March 9, 1975.

Piaget, J. *The Moral Judgement of the Child*. New York: Harcourt, Brace, 1932.

Ransom, John Crowe. "The School," *Poems About God*. New York: Halt, 1919.

Reich, Charles A. *Character Analysis, op. cit.* Introduction to 3rd edition, 1948.

Riesman, David. *The Lonely Crowd: A Study of the Changing American Character*. New Haven: Yale UP, 1950.

Robert, L.N., Chapter In Quay, H.C. and Werry, J.S. (eds.). "Psychopathological Disorders of Childhood." London: Wiley, 1972.

Rosenberg, M. Parental Interest and Chidren's Self-perceptions. *Sociometry*, 1963.

Seema, Melvin. "On the Meaning of Alienation." *American Sociological Review*, 24, 783-91, 1959.

Spivack, G. Child-rearing attitudes of emotionally disturbed adolescents. *Journal of Consulting Psychology*, 21: 178, 1957.

Stevenson, David L. "J.D. Salinger: The Mirror of Crisis." *The Nation* CLXXXIV (March 1958) 215-17.

Stewart, John L. *The Burden of Time: The Fugitives and Agrarians*. Princeton: Princeton UP, 1965.

Stinchombe, Arthur L. *Rebellion in a High School*. Chicago: Quadrangle Books, 1964.

Stone, L.J. and Church, J. *Childhood and Adolescence*. 2nd edition. New York: Random House, 1968.

Strauch, Carl F. "Kings in the Back Row: Meaning Through Structure—"A Reading of Salinger's *The Catcher in the Rye*." *Wisconsin Studies in Contemporary Literature*, II (Winter, 1961).

Tanner, Tony. *City of Words: American Fiction 1950-1970*. The Free Press, 1970.

Twain, Mark. *The Adventures of Huckleberry Finn*. New York: Harper and Brothers, 1948.

Warren, Robert Penn. "Katherine Anne Porter: Irony with a Centre." *Kenyan Review* 4 (1942) 29-42 rpt. in Katherine Anne Porter, ed. Hartley and Lane.

——. *Selected Essays*. New York: Random House, 1958.

Way, Brain. "'Franny and Zooey' and J.D. Salinger." *New Left Review*, 15 (May-June 1962).

Weiner, I.B. *Psychological Disturbances in Adolescence*. John Wiley, New York, 1970.

Welty, Eudora, "Katherine Anne Porter: A Birthday Tribute: The Eye of the Story." *Yale Review* 55 (Winter, 1966).

Wharton, Edith. *The Writing of Fiction.* New York: Scribner's, 1925.

Wiegand, William. "J.D. Salinger: Seventy-Eight Bannanas." *Chicago Review,* IX (Winter, 1958).

Wilson, H. The early diagnosis of schizophrenia. *British Medical Journal,* 1: 1502-04.

Winnicott, D.W. *The Maturational Process and the Facilitating Environment.* New York: The International UP, 1965.

Witham W. Tasker. *The Adolescent in the American Novel 1920-1960.* New York: Ungar, 1964.

Wright, Austin M. *The American Short Story in the Twenties.* Chicago: University of Chicago P, 1961.

Youth Transition to Adulthood. Report of the Panel on Youth of the President's Science Advisory Committee. Washington, D.C.: U.S. Government Printing Office, 1973.

INDEX